RI

AFTER DIVORCE

The 5 Keys For Women To Heal Wounds, Resurrect Dreams And Create A Life Full Of Love

SARA GIBBONS

Book 1

Help Your Cellves Empowerment Series

Published by Help Your Cellves

ISBN: 978-1-9993450-0-6 (Kindle)
ISBN: 978-1-9993450-1-3 (Paperback)

DEDICATION

For my mother.

ACCESS THE WEBINAR FREE!

As a thank you for buying my book I would like to give you free access to this webinar covering in person the main points of the book.

TO ACCESS GO TO:

https://www.helpyourcellves.com/free-webinar

TABLE OF CONTENTS

CHAPTER ONE

What Happened to the Fairytale?

Look good, feel good. Own your space.
– Jo Le-Rose

You are not a drop in the ocean,
you are the entire ocean in one drop.
– Rumi

If a relationship break-up has shattered you, this book was written for you, no matter what the reasons behind your break-up are.

I am going to share not only how to find peace and resolution in the aftermath of your break-up, but also how to move on and create the life you want. You might be feeling so raw that what I'm saying may seem impossible from where you are now.

I want to reassure you that it is entirely achievable. I've done it myself, and I'm going to show you how you can, too. We will go on a journey of self-discovery, so you can rise from the ashes stronger and with a greater understanding of what happened, why it happened, as well as gain a powerful sense of yourself and of your true magnificence. From here you will be able to create the life you want because simply put, you will see what you need to do to make it happen.

If this sounds too good to be true, and you feel that I can't be talking about how to move on from your particular situation, then let me clarify.

Who is This Book Written For?

If you feel you are losing hope that there is light at the end of the tunnel, let me reassure you that you really can turn things around. All I ask is that you be willing and ready to make some changes and open to looking at things a different way. As Henry Ford said, "If you always do what you've always done, you always get what you've always got." If you're ready to make room for things to shift in your life and to have a different outcome from where you are now, then you are definitely in the right place to make that a reality.

This book is for you if you feel you have lost your sense of identity, and you are looking for independence from a situation in which you feel trapped or out of control. If you are ready to accept your situation rather than fight against it and if you want to stop the pain and ups and downs of the emotional roller coaster, this book is for you. It is for you if you are afraid of repeating past patterns and getting the same result over again and if you are feeling stuck and are asking yourself, 'How can I let go of the past, forgive, and move on?'

It's very common for people to come out of a marriage asking, 'Who am I?' It can feel as if you have somehow forfeited your sense of self while together. When the relationship ends, you are left disorientated and lost. We'll be looking at why that happens and also how to change it, so you can build your self-confidence and self-esteem, and never lose your own identity again.

A break-up can also mean a lot of negativity is flying around. You want to put an end to it but can't see a way of stopping it. Again, we will be looking at how you can approach these issues with new understanding and new eyes.

If your breakup was some time ago, you might consider that while you have recovered up to a point, and life is steadier than it once was, you are still left feeling vulnerable and bruised. There are things you remain unsure about as if something is missing, something you can't quite define.

I will show you the tools you need to know to get the results you want. I have identified these from many years of personal research as well as experience from both my situation and from working with others. By following the approach here, you will be able to clarify your understanding and access your full power and potential.

We will look at:

- the importance of you and how nourishing yourself gives a greater sense of self-worth

- new understandings of what has been happening and why, so you can access the peace you crave

- the cause of why you find yourself where you are leading to both the healing of deep wounds and acceptance of your situation

- how to develop your vision for the future and create the life you want with joy

- the importance of support and how to get it, opening up to love in your life

In essence, this book is for you if you feel broken, adrift, unloved, guilty, angry, and fearful of the future. It is for you if you believe you have lost your sense of self and self-confidence. It is for you if you know there is more to life than you are experiencing and are ready to move on and access it for yourself.

You Are Not Alone

I want you to know that you are not alone in having all these painful feelings. While each person's external situation is unique, many common threads run through them. You will discover that your internal world, how you feel and think about things, your emotions, worries, and responses to your situation, is very similar to others. This is good news, as it means you can benefit from learning how others have managed to move on from the pain.

It is not unusual to feel that what happened to us is the worst. Our own experience is, of course, incredibly painful for us individually.

A while ago I had a conversation with some friends who had all experienced distressing breakups. The first said hers was the worst because her husband had left her for a younger, taller, slimmer, prettier woman, an experience that made her feel inadequate. The next said no—it was even worse to be left, as she had been, for an older, shorter and fatter woman. The third said his wife had left him for another woman, which of course was a big blow for his masculinity. The last one said they had been left for no one at all.

It was evident to all of us that, no matter what the circumstances, our confidence, and self-esteem take a huge hit. Each person had a different external experience, but internally they all felt rejected and unworthy.

For those who have initiated the breakup, there can be similar common ground often based around an element of guilt, but ultimately also coming down to self-doubt and low self-esteem. For example, you might be asking, 'If I had been different would it have happened this way?' 'Am I sure I couldn't have done more?', 'I'm lonely in the relationship, and I'm lonely out of it, how can I deal with that?' 'If they change, or if I change, would we be able to make it work?' 'I'm afraid of the consequences of leaving; I might not be able to cope' and so on. The question of whether to go or not, the yo-yo-ing, can go on for months or years.

From an early age, we are taught that if we follow the ways of society, our parents, our peers etc., we will be alright. We will be safe, secure, and everything will be ok. For example, we may have been told that if we get an education, get married, have kids, work hard, belong to a family, then we will be happy. If you are reading this because your relationship has broken up, it is likely you can already see this scenario for what it is, a whopping lie. And even if your life has followed such a pattern, you will know nothing is that simple, and there are undoubtedly limitations to the security and happiness that has been so easily promised to us.

On top of this, we've been fed a fairy tale idea of relationships, that we will meet Prince Charming, he will be The One, and when that happens, we will live happily ever after.

When a breakup happens, we question what we have been told–marriage is supposed to be for life–so why didn't that happen? What went wrong? It's not supposed to end in the turmoil of divorce. We can feel out of our depth and that no-one knows how to help us. We can think that we don't fit in, that life has become something alien; we can feel lost and very alone while also likely trying to deal with non-loving, uncooperative and potentially even damaging behaviour from our former partner. We can wonder if we will ever be able to forgive and whether our future life will be full of resentment and bitterness.

Even if we are sceptical of that fairy tale, the imprint is still deep-rooted in the mass consciousness of our society and hard to break free from, albeit if we even knew what the real-life alternative is.

Well, there is an alternative, an amazingly sustainable one, and by the end of this book, you are going to not only know what it is but also how you can make it a reality in your own life.

The guidance and insights we are going to cover in this book, have led to dramatic life changes.

'Thank you, Sara, I wouldn't be where I am,
and I couldn't have done it without you.
Thank you for what you do.'
– Michelle L, Chicago

'Shock and change can paralyse.
Sara's focus is to empower you to step into the feelings of joy, freedom, and love.'
– Patricia D, UK

'I now feel much more able to cope with the situation I am in. I feel stronger and more positive. Thank you, Sara, I am now moving forward in my new life.'
– Jenny H

My Story

But before we dive into the details of what the keys to your new life are, let me tell you something about myself.

When I first experienced my breakup, I felt utterly lost. We had been together for 16 years, and everything changed overnight. I didn't know anyone who had experienced what I was going through, and I had no help or guidance to show me the way.

I seriously thought my life was over!

I cried, read self-help books, and cried some more. We had recently moved to a new area of the country, and I had no-one to speak to about the turmoil I was in. I lost my home and my security.

I started counselling, began to get glimmers of hope, and I thought things were getting better. Then they got a whole lot worse again. I continued my searching for answers.

Over time, my old life began to fade away and a new one to emerge. Hope began. My office job was no longer a reflection of the new person that I was, so I left it and set up my own business and therapy centre. I continued to research and to train in various therapies and disciplines, and over time, the pain began to diminish and understanding and confidence to grow.

Fast forward to today, and my life looks very different from the one I had before and soon after the breakup.

I live where I have always dreamed of living, by the sea. I have abundant friends with whom I travel the world. I love my work, and it gives me financial independence. I am probably as fit and healthy as I have ever been in my life, and my confidence is where it should be. Above all, I am happy and experience real joy on a daily basis.

Now, I'm telling you all this not to brag but to assure you of what is possible. I promise you I was as low as one can be and still be on this planet. If I can turn things around, then I know 100 percent that, with the guidance here, you can, too. Not only that, you will be able to do it a whole lot faster than I did.

After my marriage breakup, I got to a pivotal point in life. I had a choice: I could stay where I was, muddle through, not make any changes, and probably end up bitter as well as stuck. Or I could let go, embrace something new, and see where it took me. I think you know already which path I chose!

As a result, I have now been a natural health practitioner and lifestyle strategist for over 20 years and have successfully helped hundreds of clients improve and move on in their lives during this time. I was the founder and owner of The Practical Natural Therapy Centre in Harrogate, UK, have worked internationally, taught classes and groups, and worked with clients individually. I have training and qualifications in counselling and nutrition, as well as in a variety of healing therapies and disciplines.

What is more important than all of this is that I have discovered how to solve my problems and those of my clients, and that is what I want to share with you now. I know there is hope, and there is always a choice, wherever or whatever your situation. You can stay stuck and watch life get smaller and smaller, or you can embrace everything it has to offer and expand it beyond what you ever thought was possible.

I have learnt that life is never over, as they say until the fat lady sings. If you are prepared to embrace the new, the unknown, and the sometimes scary, these become the exciting, the fulfilling, the joyful, and even the new familiar.

It's a beautiful world out there, and we have the gift of life to explore it and make the most of it.

It took me years to develop the skills and understanding that led to the life I have today. You can now do it in a fraction of the time it took me. I'm going to share the five essential keys you need to know to unlock your full potential and move on to the life you have always wanted and more. So don't delay, get started, and see your life unfold.

If you're ready to embrace the journey, let's get going!

CHAPTER TWO

The First Key: The Importance of *You*

He who knows others is wise.
He who knows himself is enlightened.
– Lao Tzu

Today you are You, that is truer than true.
There is no one alive who is Youer than You.
– Dr. Seuss

You have parted from your significant other, your expected life-long partner, quite possibly your soulmate, and now you find yourself asking, 'Who am I?'

All loss is potentially both painful and stressful. Numerous studies link the profound loss of a marriage to the disruption and questioning of personal identity.

If you have ever found yourself asking, 'Who am I?' then start with this answer:

'You are the most important person in your world.'

You may struggle to believe it, but by the end of this chapter, I want you to know that to be an accurate statement and be on your way to feeling it in every fibre of your being.

You are the most significant person in your world.

You are the person with whom you spend the most time.

You are most definitely and absolutely worth spending time on.

You have the gift of life, and it is yours to nourish and cherish. You are not less than anyone else (and you are not more either). It's not selfish to take time for yourself, for your personal development, and well-being. It's the opposite; it's selfish not to.

When you fly on an airplane, the demonstration before taking off emphasises that, if the cabin pressure drops, an oxygen mask will drop down for you to use. You are advised to put yours on before anyone else's. Why? Because how can you help anyone else if you don't look after yourself first?

It seems obvious, doesn't it? But we can often spend our lives putting everyone else first and then find we get sick, things go wrong, and others don't appreciate our efforts.

If you get self-care right, you align yourself with the universe, and life flows, and when life flows, everything you need follows along with it.

What Might Be Stopping You From Your Self-care?

Abraham Lincoln said, 'The best way to predict your future is to create it.'

The fact is you are already creating your future, as well as your present, but you may not have been aware of it. If you want something different, then self-care is precisely the place to start because, unless you begin to understand yourself truly, nothing much is going to change.

But, I hear someone say (and there's always a but isn't there?), but I have to look after this person, they can't do without me, I need to do this, or that or the other. There's no time for me!

So let's take a look at that.

Tough Love Alert!

Ask Yourself – Who or What am I Responsible For and Why?

Get a pen and paper and take some time to ponder this and then come back with your list.

If you feel you are responsible for anyone over 21 years old, then ask yourself why you think that.

Here's what some others have said when asked that question.

Illustration One

> Dianna's son Steven, 28, has had a fight with his girlfriend, and so has come back home to live and has brought all his belongings. The house is now overfilled, and Dianna is feeling swamped and overwhelmed. She was beginning to put her life back together after her divorce, but now she feels she has to put that on hold.
>
> Dianna could ask herself a number of questions to help her both understand the situation she finds herself in and

navigate changes in a way that enables her and her son to move forward.

For example, did Steven expect to come home without any discussion and, if so, why? How long will this be for, and how does he plan to get himself back on his feet again? Does Steven's behaviour have any echoes of his father, Dianna's ex-husband, and if so can she change her way of dealing with it? Is Steven showing her what she needs to be aware of to get the life she wants? Is she still putting what Steven feels he needs above her own needs, and if so why?

It can be hard letting loved ones find their own feet, but taking responsibility for their needs above your own will not serve either of you. A simple 'I am sure you will find a solution to this problem' on the other hand is so empowering for both of you and shows belief in their capabilities.

Illustration Two

Katrina says her work is very demanding, and that, since her divorce, she has to work long hours and has an unsympathetic boss. She needs the money, as her ex doesn't pay her support regularly. She says she doesn't have time to look after herself properly; she is too busy surviving.

There are several things Katrina could consider to help her look at this situation a little differently.

When we don't value ourselves neither does anyone else. There is always a choice. Katrina could start to make changes in small but consistent ways. Improved self-care leads to improved self-confidence, and, in turn, could mean more respect and consideration in the workplace. If it doesn't, maybe she could look for a job that better reflects her new self-respecting values or even train for work that is what she would really love to do.

If Katrina took these steps, she would also be taking responsibility for her own health and happiness as a priority. No one wants or deserves to be taken for granted or used as fodder for the employment machine in a way that has little respect for individuality and personal needs.

Both these problematic situations show an element of disrespect from others, whether intentional or not. There is little or no acknowledgement of each person's needs or wishes here. Dianna's son is not behaving as a responsible adult or viewing his mother as an adult with her own life beyond his relationship with her, preferring to slip back to child mode and expect his mother to rescue him. Katrina's boss is not recognising that she is more than someone there to solely fulfil his work demands, especially when those demands are well beyond what is reasonable to expect in employment. It is up to Dianna and Katrina to value themselves sufficiently to avoid perpetuating this type of behaviour. For a healthy relationship, you want equality. Supporting each other is excellent, one person continually carrying the burdens of another is not.

Changing this negatively enabling behaviour may come as a shock for those who think they can call on you to drop whatever you are doing and accommodate them, but it is essential for you to take back control of your own life and no longer be bounced around by the demands of others.

If you have young children, yes, of course, you need to support them and show them how to stand on their own two feet until they are young adults, but by the time they get to 18 – 21 years-old, it is time for them to be taking on responsibility for themselves.

The simple truth is we are only ultimately responsible for ourselves.

Giving others the freedom to solve their problems can be hard for those of us who have been brought up to believe that we have to be there for others. We may have been told it lacks in humanity to not do that, that family always comes first, etc.

However, we are making a distinction here between being taken for granted and being respected, between allowing others to dictate how we spend our time and taking back control of ourselves and making our own decisions.

Some people want to live their lives through others. By this I mean they put the responsibility for their own happiness onto someone else. Some parents try to live their lives through their children. Some spouses need their partner to validate them and give their life purpose and meaning. This pressure is bound to end in tears. It is not how we are meant to live. It jars against life's principles and leads to problems. We are here to live our own lives, fulfil our destinies and purpose. Yes, we can share our lives, and that is a fulfilling and enriching experience, but to give someone else the responsibility for your happiness is a burden that is either too much for them to bear or opens you up to manipulation and emotional blackmail.

Joan's second marriage had broken up, and she was finding it much harder to get over than the first. She turned to her grown sons for support and attention. While they were sympathetic at first, they also both had families and busy lives of their own and found her demands excessive and uncomfortable. They felt Joan depended on them too much, and it was causing friction in their own families and with their wives.

When Joan told her sons they were her only reason for living now that her marriage had ended, she didn't realise what a heavy burden she was placing on them to please her. She was shocked when they both distanced themselves from her. The more they pulled away, the more Joan piled on the emotional pressure, and, as a consequence, her sons withdrew further until there was no communication at all.

Cut off entirely from her sons and grandchildren, Joan was even more devastated. She courageously sought help, and, over time, came to see and understand what she was doing. As she realised that her happiness was her decision, Joan also started to feel better about herself. It was critical for her to understand her life wasn't over and that she wasn't dependent on her sons or, for that matter, on having a husband, for life to have meaning and for her to be fulfilled.

Keeping Everyone Happy

Many people spend a lot of time and energy trying to please others. The reasons for this include trying to avoid conflict, manipulating to get a wanted result, an attempt to make things alright for someone, or to be thought well of by others. You probably already know you can't please all the people all of the time, and to try to do so is often ultimately at our own expense.

You may have beliefs that tell you that others are more important than you and that you must put others first. When you start to question this, you are another step closer to fully knowing that you are the most significant person in your world.

Does Putting Myself and Self-care First Mean I Will Be Selfish and Lonely?

If looking after yourself and putting yourself at the top of the list feels like it will isolate you from others, understand that nothing could be further from the truth.

When you care for yourself, when you feel sure of your strength and power when you are healthy, joy-filled, and living a vibrant life, what do you think will happen? Your friendship group will grow and develop, your life will expand, and your self-worth will continue to expand with it. There will be opportunities you never before dreamed of coming your way.

Dealing with Reluctance

It may be that even after all we have just covered, self-care is the last place you want to start because you want to fix all those pressing problems and anxieties that are making life a misery. Won't feelings of peace and joy and happiness follow after that? The truth is life works the other way around.

Change for the better happens when you take your primary focus off attending to the external and instead giving priority to you and what you are creating with your actions, feelings, thoughts, and words.

How quickly that change happens is, therefore, in your hands, under your control. If there is something new to be aware of and grasp, something that you perhaps need to change or accept, you can either adapt to it the first time it appears, or the 2nd, the 22nd or the 222nd. The choice is yours. You have the power.

Tough Love Alert!

It is a life principle that we attract to us what we need for our lives to grow and expand, and it will keep on coming to us until we see it for what it is and take action to make the needed changes.

Melissa said the times in her life that she felt the most hurt were when she was not validated and approved of in her marriage by her two ex-husbands. When she said that she also perceived herself as unapproved of by her boss, despite all her qualifications and skills, she began to see there was a pattern emerging concerning her self-perception and approach to feeling validated.

Instead of the problem being the behaviour of the people in her life, she began to recognise that she was seeking approval from them because she didn't feel worthy or approve of herself.

Seeing this lack of worth in herself was a light bulb moment. Recognising that the more approval she sought from others the less was received, Melissa realised that each person was reflecting her belief of not being worthy back to her. Then she knew where to focus her attention.

In hindsight, Melissa could see that she had previously been reluctant even to contemplate that it was her lack of self-value that was causing her so many problems.

She started to listen more openly in difficult situations, rather than quickly responding defensively, and to try to be as honest as she could to see what her part in it was. If there was something to accept, then she would aim to take it on board, and, if there wasn't, she'd let it go as another's issue. The bonus here is that, as she stopped reacting negatively to her boss and stayed in the growing knowledge of her self-worth and abilities, her boss's attitude also changed, and work became much less of a chore. She will probably never be best buddies with her boss, but their relationship is now a lot easier and more straightforward.

It took Melissa a while to fully realise that it was her lack of self-value being shown to her by others in her life not validating her. As a result, she is now much more confident that her next intimate relationship will not follow the same route as the last two. She has broken the mould.

While you can't change something unless you are aware of it, when you are aware, understand, and as a result, respond and react differently, then you don't have to experience that anymore. This change in the reaction is where we stop repeating the patterns of the past. As a result, this is where you can make your own choices and move on.

Have a look at where you are holding back, where you are reluctant to change, and where you are avoiding the new.

Gently acknowledge this is what you are doing, but then give it no more power. It can be challenging and a bit scary at first, but the gains are enormous.

Now that you are aware of some of the things that can affect your self-worth and, as a result, stop your self-care, let's have a look at some practical things you can do straight away to help yourself feel better.

Self-care: Some Practical Pointers

Make Some Space

Have nothing in your house that you do not know to be useful, or believe to be beautiful.
– William Morris

We are living in a time when many of us in western society have more possessions and belongings than ever before. It is likely that we have more things in the house than we need. There are those just-in-case items. Maybe the handy little pots that could well come in useful sometimes. Or not. Perhaps there are the keys you've had in that drawer for years that you may find out what it is they unlock at some point. Someone told me she found 15 cans of fly spray when clearing out her mother's house, and ten years later, they've just used up the last one! There are the held onto, unmatched items like socks or earrings, whose partner may turn up, but most likely won't.

You need space to take action to get your life where you want it to be. There has to be some wriggle room you can leverage.

Physical clutter leads to mental clutter, and there are considerable benefits to streamlining your own space.

Start with your bedroom, and move on and out anything you do not truly love or need. Make the room somewhere special for you so that it's your sanctuary, somewhere you can take a break from the world and recharge the batteries. Clear out the cupboards and wardrobes, clean everywhere, repaint if needed. You are creating a space for you.

The effects of decluttering can be significant. You are working on reclaiming you and where better to start than your most personal, intimate space. Keep it private. It's just for you and no-one else unless you have young children. Even if you have little ones, you can still show them how to respect your space as they grow, just as they will want you to respect theirs, particularly when the teenage times arrive. Mutual respect is an excellent starting place for those potentially tricky years.

After you have finished your bedroom, you can bit by bit work your way through any other bedrooms and then the rest of the house, including the garage and shed if you have them.

If you're highly motivated to make big changes, then doing this fast will facilitate that. However, I realise this may seem a daunting task if your life is already super busy with commitments and activities, but if you do it steadily and consistently, taking action step by step over the time you need, the rewards you find will be enormous and the ideas we will be exploring later so much easier to implement. Throwing out your physical clutter means you can more easily throw out the emotional clutter too. It means you can say goodbye to the old habits and patterns and ways of thinking, as well as old regrets and resentments, and move to the future instead of being repeatedly being sucked back to the past by the memories and associations.

Making Lists and Keeping a Journal

I highly recommend you make a list of all the things you need to do and put yourself and self-care (including some clearing and decluttering) at the top. You at the top is non-negotiable. That is how valuable you are.

Making a list can help you both prioritise and avoid overwhelm. Tick things off as you go, and add others in as you need to. A list enables you to be accountable and makes sure you optimise the use of your time. If you don't know what to do next, go to your list!

I also strongly recommend you keep a journal. It can be beneficial to write out all your thoughts and worries as part of clearing out the old, and we will go into that in more detail in Chapter 4. You can also have a separate journal for all your insights and learnings and even a third if you want for your confirmations and the evidence you glean that you are on the right path.

It can be so helpful to look back on these stepping stones you are taking. You can use your journals to help keep you on track and also as encouragement as you see how far you've come and grown.

My own journals are full of insights, breakthrough moments, and ideas as well as confirmations for me. They are a fantastic resource to look at when I feel I need inspiration or a reminder of what I have done in the past. It is not unusual for me to see something I had completely forgotten about but is very pertinent to my life now. Sometimes we need reminders of things we thought we had already learnt as well as encouragement in seeing what we have worked through in the past and the benefits we are now experiencing. That makes appreciation and gratitude grow, and the circle is complete. Then around we can go again, expanding into more growth, more understandings, more benefits, and more appreciation.

Eat Well and Keep Hydrated, Take Regular Exercise

It is essential to eat well, to give your body proper nutrition and to stay well hydrated. That isn't to say you never have a treat or a glass of something lovely again. What it does mean though is valuing yourself enough to get the balance right, to nourish all the hard-working magical little cells of your body.

Our bodies are designed to move. A sedentary lifestyle can lead to low mood as well as health issues. Some people like to go to the gym; some want to jog. That's fine, but it's not necessary or indeed the only way to keep in shape. Walking is fantastic exercise, as is Pilates, Yoga or Tai Chi. Starting gently and being consistent is better than going in hard and then giving up. Please, no heroics! And do consult your physician if you have any health concerns and before you start a new health and fitness programme.

Stress and Relaxation

Stress is a significant factor in poor health and well-being. On a purely physical level, it increases toxins in the body and gives our precious hard-working little cells so much more to do. It also affects mood and levels of positivity etc., thus affecting our mental and emotional health both directly and indirectly.

Stress occurs when we have feelings of not being able to cope with what we believe we must do to survive simultaneously with feelings of negativity and overwhelm with regard to our ability to accomplish what we need to. To start dealing with stress, you may need to review your perceived responsibilities and needs and your attitude about them. Not taking timely action, in other words procrastinating, can also lead to stress as things build up. There is always a choice about how we spend our time and energy, even if it is a tough one. Remember, your own health must be top of the list.

In my work as a health coach, I often find people underestimate the significance of stress in the development of illness in the body. We can't always control what happens to us but what we can do is master our responses.

A 'fight or flight' response is triggered by stress. In effect this means stress is asking us to either resolve the situation as far as possible by taking action, or to recognise that it's something we can't affect and so relax through it and thereby tell the body 'Thank you for the warning, I've heard you and there's no need for the warning anymore'. If we ignore the signal and don't take the action needed, then small things become bigger things, until aches pains and more serious illness develops.

The resolution involves both mind and body, which is why self-care must always be at the top of the list, and mastering relaxation is essential.

If you are feeling stressed and need to relax more, here are some things to try:

- Meditation
- Slow, deep breathing
- Walks in nature, by the sea, on grass, through forests, etc.
- Mindfulness–bringing yourself to the present moment.
- Tai Chi/Chi Gong or Yoga
- Take action in the moment. Avoid putting things off.

If you want more detail on practical steps for health and well-being, go to www.helpyourcellves.com/free-resources

I want to emphasise how important it is not to get overwhelmed by the suggestions here. You are not expected or even encouraged to do everything at once. Manageable and consistent steps are the way forward. Above all, be kind and gentle with yourself, and always give yourself the compassion you would want another to show to you and that you would show to another.

Self-care results in improved health, strength and fitness, improved mood, refreshed emotional wellbeing, and greater mental clarity. In essence, you will feel better, have more inner resources, and be better at decision making. All of these will go a long way towards improving your self-esteem and self-confidence.

Commit to honouring yourself daily because you are the most important and significant person in your world. Focusing on you as your starting point plays a massive part in getting yourself unstuck. It stops the downward spiral of mood, and it gives you energy for the next essential steps.

Summary

- You are important, the most important person in your world. You have value.
- It is respectful to that value to give yourself the priority you deserve.
- When you give yourself priority, you align yourself with the universe.
- When you align yourself with the universe, your life flows.
- You are only responsible for yourself.
- Pleasing others is at the expense of you.
- Difficult situations are an opportunity for growth into the life you want.

Main Action Steps

1. Make space for the new by decluttering your physical space.
2. Utilise lists – with you at the top – to keep you on track.

3. Start a journal (or three), for writing out worries, to remind you of your new insights, and keep track of the evidence you are on the right path.

4. Practice physical self-care, eating well, exercise, and relaxation.

5. Be consistent and learn to acknowledge baby steps as progress.

The Result

You will experience reclamation of self-worth and self-identity.

CHAPTER THREE

The Second Key: Be Open to Seeing with New Eyes

It's no use going back to yesterday
because I was a different person then.
– Lewis Carroll

Life is like riding a bicycle.
To keep your balance, you must keep moving.
– Albert Einstein

In the previous chapter we've looked at the importance of putting yourself at the top of your own priority list, knowing you have value and recognising the need to give yourself bucket loads of care and attention. Now you are in a place where you are ready to see what else you can do to keep the momentum going.

Earlier we touched on the significant link between stress and a healthy body. In this chapter, we will look in more detail at some areas that cause that emotional stress and how you can look at them a little differently. This, in turn, will help you respond to the changes in a way that will set you firmly on your path to emotional freedom as well as better health. These are the aspects that stop you moving on unless they are addressed. For this reason, we are going to dive deep into the messiness, looking at stumbling blocks that have likely been tripping you up and keeping you stuck. It's time to kick them into touch.

Acknowledge Where You Are

I have spoken to many for whom the sudden and unexpected end of a relationship brings about profound shock. A world turned upside down and a life no longer heading in the direction you had come to expect is a lot to take in. The shock can be followed by disbelief and denial regarding what is truly happening. Then occurs the reaction.

Some people decide to take action straight away and remove themselves from the situation in an attempt to practically and emotionally be finished with everything as quickly as possible. They want to put the past behind them and move on feeling there is nothing more to be done, said or looked at.

Others try to understand what has happened. This attempt might be accompanied by a reluctance to accept the end, a bid to try to see if the relationship can be salvaged, and they may perhaps enter into lengthy talks and negotiations.

Each situation is unique, but the emotional heartbreak still needs to be dealt with, and the shock and fallout can reverberate for months, years, and even decades. It's not easy to draw a healthy line to mark the end of a previously committed relationship.

For those whose marriage has been moving slowly and painfully to its inevitable termination for a while, there can still be shock as the ending of the relationship unfolds. The grief at the dissolution of the optimism with which the relationship began, the loss of dreams and expectations, can be hard to accept.

Tough Love Alert!

Acknowledge Life Is Going To Be Different

The first step to moving on is to face the fact that, wherever the situation goes and whatever happens, life is not going to be the same again. It may sound obvious. It is also true that this is the point where many get stuck and stay in a failing relationship for much longer than they needed to, causing much additional pain and stress. It is a desperate desire to hold onto the familiar, the comfortable, and the known that causes the anguish and anxiety. Hence, the tough love alert.

The Blunt Choice:

> Resist the fact that life is in the process of changing with or without your permission and thereby stay in the pain, anxiety, and feelings of loss,
>
> or
>
> Let go of the need to control the situation or anyone else, move towards embracing change, which in turn will lead to new perspectives and also open doors for you that you didn't even know were there or were possible.

If you genuinely want to stop the pain, then the second step is essential. I know it's unlikely that you will feel you can do that all in one go. Very few of us have been taught from childhood how to manage change comfortably, and it can take some adjusting on many levels to adopt a new and different view of life. This is why the rest of this chapter will be looking in more depth at how you can handle as well as grow from various aspects of this new situation you find yourself in. If you are willing to make moves towards choice two, you will see results. Otherwise, not much of what we are going to cover now will have meaning or make sense. And for those seeking closure in their relationship, then embracing the new is essential.

It's a fact of life that you are the only person you can change; you cannot change another. When you begin to grasp this and take action for yourself, it results in changes around you because now you are getting more aligned with how life works. In other words, you are working with universal laws and not habitual patterns that don't serve you.

Are you in?

We are going on a journey which puts you firmly back in the driving seat of your life, where you understand the principles of living and, as a result, know how to create what you want rather than have things randomly happen to you.

If you're still reading, I'll take that as a yes. Yay!

Tough Love Alert!

(I know they're coming thick and fast now, but it will get easier. I promise!)

Putting Yourself Centre Stage

We have already spoken in the previous chapter about the importance of self-care to build your self-esteem alongside good energy levels and a healthy body. We said this would help you make sound decisions as you move on and have mental clarity as well as generally feeling good.

Now we are going to look deeper at what is happening to you emotionally because unless you address this, it can both undermine you and bring you down.

The fact that you are reading this book means it is likely you are finding yourself not only in a difficult situation but also involved in some dramas, as you try to navigate your way through it all. Whatever has happened, however dreadful it has all been, the only person who can get you out of your situation is you. Others can point the way, but they can't take the action that you need to undertake for yourself. A caring parent teaches their children to find their independence and shows them the consequences of their actions when they are going off track. Similarly, if we want to live well as adults, we have to be prepared to continue to change and grow throughout our lives as we understand more about ourselves and deal with complex issues.

I am not condoning unacceptable or damaging behaviour here. But it is essential to recognise that we don't have to play the victim role. The easy way is to blame others for where we find ourselves. However, that will keep us stuck and is the equivalent of falling off that bicycle that must keep moving to stay upright. If we want to move on, then we have to take some action. The trick here is to know what action to take and when.

There is no standing still. We either have a life that grows and expands, or our life diminishes and gets smaller.

You have probably seen older people whose world gets smaller and more restricted as they age. Their fears become increasingly apparent; their life becomes limited in an attempt to keep themselves safe. These changes can happen so gradually, by a series of mini-decisions taken over many years, that it seems reasonable to them. They feel that's just the way life is, that random things happen and that these things seem to get scarier as life goes on. The UK comedian Peter Kay joked that his grandma had to leave the family wedding party at 5 pm to go home and close the curtains.

By contrast, you have a tremendous opportunity in front of you now as a result of what has happened. You can take steps to understand it and why. You can ensure you don't find yourself in the same situation again. You can turn your life around in ways you never thought possible despite feeling stuck in a downward spiral. Yes, you may have had an enormous shock. For myself, I needed that shock to get me to see where my life was heading without it. Whatever has happened to you, the more you understand and the more you apply that understanding by taking action, the smoother your life is going to become. Of course, there will be challenges, but you will develop tools to handle them, and life won't seem so random.

Let's go a little deeper and see what you can do about it.

What Roles Do You Play?

After a breakup, troublesome exchanges that happened within the marriage tend to get even trickier.

The Karpman triangle is a way of looking at the roles taken in a relationship drama, so you can better see what is happening and develop ways to step off the cycle.

PERSECUTOR
The Bad One
"I'm right"
Blames others for problems

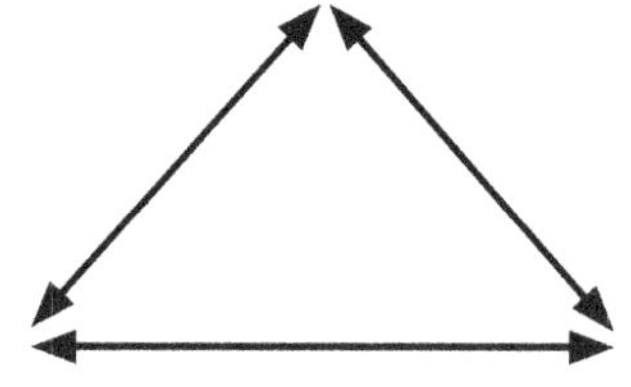

RESCUER
The Good One
"Poor you"
Gains self-esteem
by helping others

VICTIM
The Powerless One
"Poor me"
Dependent on others
to solve their problems

The Karpman Triangle

The 'victim' (V) role is the poor me, the person who feels oppressed, hopeless, and unable to make decisions. The payoff in taking on this role is to feel justified in blaming another for the situation rather than solving one's own problems.

The victim will attribute their situation to the actions of 'persecutor' (P), the bad guy, the bully, who is oppressive, controlling, and superior. The persecutor is happy to allocate blame, to let others know they are in the wrong. The payoff for them is feeling self-righteous and justified.

The rescuer (R) wants to help. They feel guilty if they don't, but the effect of the rescuer on the victim he or she tries to save is that the victim continues to feel unable to solve things for themselves, which in turn keeps them dependent. The benefit for the rescuer is that by helping others, they don't have to look at the issues that they need to solve for themselves.

Do any of these roles sound familiar? Once you recognise them you'll see them everywhere!

It is also a typical pattern in a relationship drama for the roles to change and for the players to take on different parts in a scenario. Here's a simple example to illustrate.

> **Mary:** "I can't believe you've missed seeing your time with the children again."(P)
>
> **Sam:** "Well I had to work longer, as Peter's wife was sick, and I was needed to cover for him." (R)
>
> **Mary:** "You are always the one who does cover, you need to stand up for yourself, and let someone else do their bit too." (P)
>
> **Sam:** "You wouldn't want me to get out of favour with my boss, would you? I might lose my job." (V)
>
> **Mary:** "You could suggest that Mark does some of the extra, or that you could do it at home sometimes." (R)

Sam: "You have no idea how it works in our place, you've got it all wrong!" (P)

And so on.

The argument goes around and around until someone moves out of the triangle into healthier communication. Here are a few examples of how to do this.

The persecutor can move from bullying into challenging mode instead. For example, Mary could say, "I am willing to listen to why you missed seeing the children."

The victim can move from helpless to problem-solving for themselves. Sam could say, "I will discuss this in the office to see if there's any way my workload can take account of my new domestic arrangements, so I can spend time with my children regularly."

The rescuer can move from solving others problems and keeping victim dependent to coaching and supporting. Mary could say, "I'm sure you'll be able to find a way you can work things out with your colleagues that will solve the problem."

It can be uncomfortable to observe the roles of victim, rescuer, and persecutor in yourself and realise what you have been doing. Remember there is no judgement in this, you are simply waking up to what is really going on. Congratulate yourself on your increasing awareness. This is the first step to making changes, so seeing what is really happening is a huge step forward.

Once you are able to see the roles you play, when you recognise where you are on the cycle, you can get yourself out of it. Taking action to step off the cycle means you no longer have to endlessly revisit the same problems and issues with the same results.

Ending the Self-blame, Guilt, and Regrets

'How much do we need to let go of?'
a friend asked one day.
I'm not certain, 'I replied, 'but maybe ***everything****.'*
– Melody Beattie

We all know what it is like to feel bad about something that's happened in our lives, and often no more so than when facing the end of a long-term relationship. Whether initiated or not, whether someone else is involved or not, the loss of our dreams and the fear that we may well have played a part in their demise, as well as anxiety for the unknown future, can be anything from uncomfortable to paralysing. Feeling guilty and blaming ourselves undermines our self-worth, confidence, and self-esteem. We regret what happened; we wish we'd acted or said things differently. We give ourselves a hard time because we judge ourselves as bad.

For someone to be guilty, there also has to be blame somewhere. In other words, someone has to have been considered to have done something wrong.

So, let's take this step by step.

For example:

Are you not happy about something? Have you done something you feel has caused a problem for someone or created a situation that leaves you feeling guilty and uncomfortable?

If yes, do you feel that you would act differently were you in that situation again?

Can you do something to make amends, if appropriate? Perhaps a sincere verbal or written acceptance of your role in the situation is in order.

If you have done what you can and felt to be your best, has the situation been amended or resolved? If yes, that's great. Now you can let it go. If not, let it go anyway. It's over. If you have done the external action that needed doing, then that's the end of it. Now it's time to let it go internally, to release it from within you and move on.

This level of honesty with yourself will also help you face situations more realistically and help you see what has been happening between you and your ex-partner.

Again, letting go doesn't mean condoning unacceptable behaviour in another, but it does involve acknowledgement of the facts of the situation, and also recognising that the only person you can change is yourself. To try to do anything else will only drive you nuts. You'll have to accept that at some point, so it's a great idea to do it up front. I promise you; there is a huge relief when this happens, *huge*. It is like having a weight lifted from you.

It's the holding on that gives us pain and causes distress. Some people are so laid back nothing much bothers them; they take life as it comes, are positive in their outlook, and they roll with any blows. How many people do you know who are genuinely laid back and distressed? It's just not possible, is it? So, take a good look at what you are holding onto–and know that this is what is causing you pain in some form or another. When you can recognise this for what it is, let it go, and bring yourself back to the present. You are then on your way to mastering yourself and how you feel no matter what the circumstances.

No more guilt. No more self-blame. You are doing your best, and I want you to know you are not a bad person because your relationship is breaking up. You are moving towards being able to accept the situation as a fact and understand that there are steps you can take to move past the pain.

You possibly want to know how you got to where you are in the first place, and how can you make sure it doesn't happen again.

Here are a few things to look at. See if they resonate with you and the way you feel about yourself.

Why Another Can Never Complete Us

Looking to another to complete you is where there is emotional or psychological reliance on a partner to feel secure, worthy, or fulfilled.

Reliance is often a mutual aspect of an ongoing relationship. For example, you may notice that an outgoing personality will tend to attract a more introverted person, or a scattered person may go for a more steadying partner. A bully will look for a submissive person, and an unsure person may search for strength in another (who then may turn out to be a bully).

There is a tendency to look for another to fill in the gaps where there are feelings, conscious or subconscious, of not being complete or whole, or where there is a feeling that there are some characteristics or features missing or underdeveloped. Someone who perhaps feels disorganised and loses opportunities because of it may well seek a more organised partner. The more organised partner may welcome the greater spontaneity the other shows, perhaps aware that being over organised has its pitfalls by limiting what life can offer in the moment.

In this simple example, while both are happy with this situation, they will get on well. But what tends to happen over time is that the organised person will begin to tire of the unreliability of the more scattered one, and the scattered one starts to resent being organised by another.

As this situation continues, there are three choices.

1. It can get too much, and they will separate, deciding to look for a better match. Though by not addressing the underlying issues, the situation will most likely repeat itself in one form or another.

2. They can try to ride the upsets as they happen, and push the issues under the carpet. This denial can seemingly work well for a time. But there will be a build-up of resentment, and, as a result, there will quite probably be times when the situation explodes.

3. The third option is for both partners to look honestly at themselves and where they are seeking completeness in another

> (and then in turn also resenting it). If both change, adapt, and grow from it, becoming complete in themselves and not needing another to balance them, their relationship will develop into a more enriching one. They will be in a more fulfilling relationship that includes greater acceptance of one another.

When you are ready for another partner, rather than looking for the other person to make you complete, you will surely want to be a whole, vibrant, resourceful person in your own right. When you can become that person, you will attract another with the same completeness for an equitable and healthy relationship.

For some, it is a scary prospect to be such an independent person, particularly for those who may have been in a marriage for decades. But you can do it. And you are meant to do it. We will look together at how you can make this a reality.

Why It Is Important To Take Responsibility For Yourself

In Chapter Two we looked at why you are only responsible for yourself (plus young children and pets if you have them) and how important it is to put yourself and your self-care at the top of your priority list.

For people who are naturally very caring, this can be a hard one to come to terms with and to find a healthy balance. Those close to you, family, friends, partners, ex-partners know you well. They likely know how to push those buttons that trigger you to take the action they want. You can feel manipulated and used. Manipulation is a sort of emotional blackmail, and when it happens, it's time to look at that guilt again that we spoke of earlier.

Let's turn it around and look at it another way.

Tough Love Alert!

If you allow others to make demands on you that you are not entirely comfortable with or that limit you, and, if you then take action because you feel you ought to or if you think you're the only person that can really help, then you may want to take a step back and reassess.

Martha and Simon were high school sweethearts who married young and had a family soon after. Simon was the breadwinner and Martha the homemaker, but when Simon suddenly announced after 30 years together that he wanted a divorce and quickly, Martha was wholly blindsided and could not think straight; she felt as if her whole world was rocked, and all her fears came bubbling to the surface.

Martha had spent her entire life caring for her husband and children, knew nothing else, and felt she had no other skills. Martha was also shocked to find out a few months later that Mark had a new girlfriend, with whom he was doing all the things she had hoped they would do together. But the biggest bombshell was that Mark was no longer the same person towards her. Martha felt she didn't know him anymore. She had lost her precious family life and her best friend in one go.

After being dedicated entirely to her husband and family, it took a massive effort for Martha to pick up the pieces and rebuild her life. She came to realise that she had sacrificed herself, her identity, and her life dreams to provide a family life that she thought was her duty and expected of her. Martha understood that, at some point in her marriage, a line had been crossed from being both a loving wife and a person in her own right to being subservient to the family's needs. She had taken on the role of trying to solve everyone's problems to keep the family happy.

After the initial trauma when she blamed herself, Martha began to see that it wasn't her fault that the marriage had ended. She didn't need to take responsibility for Mark's actions. He had to do that. Martha knew she had done her best as far as she knew at that time, but by tracing the expectations and beliefs that had guided her life back to their source, she discovered that it is possible to do things differently.

Martha realised that her life wasn't over but instead that it was a new chapter unfolding. Things began to take a positive change in direction, as she started to do things just for herself, discovered new facets of herself in the process, and as a result, became more self-sufficient as a person, no longer so dependent on the approval of others. Her self-esteem grew, and the feeling of duty was evaporating.

She also realised that, while Mark may have left anyway, at least if she'd followed her dreams as well as bringing up her family, she could have had a more expanded and fulfilling life. She is now focusing on making that a reality for herself.

Martha's story is by no means unique. I have heard many variations of it over the years. The main thing is to know that it is never too late. Ever. Taking responsibility means you can set a new course for your life, and the best time to do that is now.

You can let go of the 'what if's'. The past is gone. Yes, of course, there will be some sadness that things have not worked out the way that you wanted. However, those who have been through the trauma of divorce and taken action to put themselves back on track in their lives will tell you life after a breakup has the potential to be better than you ever expected and is quite likely to be better than it was before.

If that seems too far away for you and the grief and sense of loss is still overwhelming, then have a look at the exercise on 'Celebrating Loss' by going to the free resources section of my website.

www.helpyourcellves.com/free-resources

This exercise encourages you to take time for yourself to both fully feel your loss but also, just as important, to honour what you had together. It is a powerful tool.

Know that people who love and take responsibility for themselves draw in more love into their lives. It's a universal law, the law of attraction. Taking action to move things onward is going to come back to you multiplied. It is so worth the effort.

Master Your Emotions To Avoid Overwhelm and Find Peace

There are going to be times when it all seems too much, and you can find yourself slipping into anxiety and even depression from the sense of being swamped by the changes that are happening. The peace you yearn for seems light years away and impossible to reach.

We are generally not taught from childhood how to deal with our emotions, so we can be at a loss when they then become overwhelming. Not fully experiencing feelings at the time they occur leads to problems because they can get stuck. When this happens, we can feel low and miserable. We need to get in contact with the emotions and feel through them as they arise.

Depression is often linked to suppressed emotion.

Sometimes people say to me they are afraid the crying will never stop. Many are also scared to open themselves to their feelings, as they are too painful. What you need to ask yourself is what is more painful? To explore the emotions and let them move through you and dissipate relatively quickly, or to block them and feel the stuckness and misery over weeks, months, or even years?

If you feel helpless or hopeless, have a look for the emotions beneath that. They will be there. You may need to find a private place to scream, shout, and release the feelings of anger, even rage, that is often behind it. Talk it out, shout it out, write it out, but whatever you do, get it out! You will feel so much better afterwards and will have taken some more steps to move on. Well done.

One final word on feeling down. Some years ago I was given advice that I have found to be a useful rule of thumb guideline on those miserable feelings when you start to worry if it will ever end.

If you are feeling low, but your mood goes up and down over 24 hours, then focus on dealing with the feelings as they arise as we have spoken about above.

However, if you are feeling very low and desperate, and, if you continuously stay that way with absolutely no relief for 24 hours or more, then this is when you may want to speak to someone and get some additional help.

Once you learn to master expressing and experiencing your feelings in the moment, you will begin to find that there is a wonderful sense of peace that follows.

Getting a Handle On Feelings of Rejection

For those whose partner left them for another, do you remember the four people I told you about in Chapter 1? They all felt their situation was the worst. One person's partner left them for a younger woman, one for an older woman, one man was left for another woman, and another for no one at all.

The common theme here is the loss of self-esteem, and this has happened in the perception of having been rejected. All these people felt low, unworthy, and lacking in confidence. In other words, the presence of a spouse or long-term partner was consciously or subconsciously being considered an indication of their worth.

That there is a need to be in a couple to have value is a widespread perception. There is a belief that we are not whole, not complete, not quite right if we don't have a partner. Our peers and others often want to see us settled and happy with a partner. It can be hard being single when so much in society is geared up to couples.

It is useful to change perspective and look at the situation in a completely different way.

Tough Love Alert!

Is it the truth that you are being rejected OR has your former partner exercised their freedom to make a different choice?

As adults, we are only responsible for ourselves. That is just as true for your ex as it is for you. If someone chooses to do something different, that is their responsibility. I know they are breaking their marriage vows, but people do have the option in our society to do that. We may not like the decision or the repercussions it has on us and all those around, but it is still their freedom to make that choice. Your choice, your freedom, is to decide how you are going to respond and how you are going to move on with your life.

We come back to that by now familiar theme.

You cannot change another. You can only change yourself.

If someone makes a choice we don't like, it doesn't mean we are at fault or unworthy or that we have to get lost in feelings of rejection or low self-esteem. It doesn't say we are wrong in any way; it merely means we are no longer, at least in our ex's eyes, a good fit for each other. If one of the partners feels this way, then there is surely no point in prolonging the pain.

When overwhelming feelings of the rejection/not good enough variety come up, go back to self-care. Self-care will raise your self-worth and confidence again. Remember, self-care means making yourself your number one priority, so caring for ourselves means doing the exact opposite of what feelings of unworthiness tell us to do. Practising self-care really is rinse and repeat, rinse and repeat, rinse and repeat until you have changed the habitual negative feelings to healthy ones that support your self-esteem.

Why Did He Cheat?

We can't leave the subject of rejection without a word on infidelity. It's likely more common than we know because cheaters hide their behaviour and the one being cheated on is either unaware or feels so confused, ashamed or frightened by the consequences they keep silent.

There are two main reasons why people cheat. The first is to be rescued, the other is to rescue another. Both involve looking externally for something that is missing in their life, rather than internally. If someone is unhappy in a relationship, instead of working out why they are unhappy and making the changes needed, they are looking outside themselves for the answer. They look to another to make their life what they want it to be. Which is why people can be serial cheaters; in practice, it's actually serial avoidance of looking at the self.

For example, if a man feels his needs aren't being met, he may cheat and leave his wife for another. Perhaps he feels his wife cares more for the children and gives them more attention than she does him. He will have been consciously or subconsciously looking for someone who will rescue him and give him the attention he craves that he feels he does not get at home.

In another scenario, a man may leave because he considers he has no role in the family. He may reckon that life will carry on just fine without him, that he is not valued. He finds another who gives him the validation he seeks by maybe putting him on a pedestal as her Prince Charming. He feels he is playing an important role by being critically significant in her life. It will satisfy his desperate need to find his self-worth and self-justification from helping another.

I'm not saying either of these scenarios describe what is factually happening in the family home; it's all about how we feel. If someone has feelings of being overlooked, they may be drawn to someone else in the hope of being rescued by them and given the attention they desire. If someone feels what they have to offer is underappreciated, then there will be a temptation to leave for someone who they consider needs what they have to offer.

Jack had closely linked his self-esteem to being the primary breadwinner in their family. When his wife's career took off suddenly and she started to earn significantly more than he did, he felt severely undermined and that she had no time for him anymore. She was busy at work, and they had less time to talk and be together than previously. Jack felt sidelined. He started to see a junior at his office who was in turn attracted to Jack's outgoing personality and was flattered someone of Jack's position in the company would be interested in her. She gave him the ego boost he felt he was missing at home.

Serial cheaters are those who, by the very act of wanting to either be rescued by someone or seek someone to rescue, are looking for a way to build up their sense of self-worth. They don't feel good about themselves; they see the relationship as the cause and want to know if it is possible to find the feeling they are searching for elsewhere and with someone else.

I want this to be very clear for all you dear ones feeling broken by cheating. You are not responsible for another's behaviour.

That's not to say you can sit back though and feel justified to blame, because it's also true you chose each other. I know that's a tough one to acknowledge! The way out and up though is to take an honest look at ourselves, our behaviour and patterns, and really value ourselves.

That is exactly what we are doing here with the five keys. We are looking at how you can rescue yourself. When you improve your sense of self, when you have a healthy self-identity, you will attract another who similarly has a strong sense of self and with whom being rescued or rescuing plays no part.

Jealousy: When the Green-eyed Monster Raises Its Head

A quick mention here about jealousy because it is likely to destroy any relationship in its path. Sometimes, especially initially, jealousy is confused with love and seen as a sign of seriousness and commitment. In truth, it's a sign of insecurity. It reflects seeing the other as someone to be possessed, which of course is disrespectful and demeaning.

In a jealous relationship, there is little or no room for trust or personal growth and development. It is a prison caused by fear and insecurity which, like a parasite, eventually destroys its host. To love is to accept, and allow freedom of choice.

If you are a jealous person, then the place to look is at your insecurity. All the things we are speaking about here concerning self-care, being complete in yourself, and changing ourselves as opposed to looking to change others are very relevant. As you resolve your fears and expand your life, you will no longer need the false comfort blanket of trying to control another to meet your needs.

If you like the idea of someone being possessive over you, then look at your need to be loved and for someone else to take care of you, even at the expense of your freedom. The key to your freedom is self-knowledge and will not be found in another.

Silencing the Destructive Power of Judgement and Opinions

Whenever a significant event like divorce happens, the effects ripple out widely to family and friends. It also means there is rarely a shortage of opinions on what you should be doing and how you should be doing it. Many people are quick to take sides, and this can be painful. Friends can behave unexpectedly in these different circumstances, and friendship groups can change too.

Just as we said another's choices have nothing to do with you (even if it feels like rejection) neither do their opinions and judgements. Any judgement says everything about the person doing the judging.

Why does someone judge? To make themselves feel better. They judge so that in comparison to another they look and feel better. In other words, the motivation, whether done consciously or not, is from their low self-esteem.

Genuine confidence and personal power come from the acceptance of self and acceptance of others.

Setting aside judgements and opinions can be an immense mindset change because so much in our society, the media, soap operas, reality shows, social media, and politics, for example, is based on the assumption that it is OK to criticise others who are not the same as us, or not doing what we feel they should be. Many families have this assumption as the norm too, discussing others behaviour and having opinions about what they do and whether it is right or wrong. If you have a family like this, you are quite likely to see it as normal, even if it is painful when you are the object of discussion.

If you worry about what your family or friends think, this will affect your ability to listen to your feelings about what you want to do. Learning to see your concerns about others opinions of you and step aside takes effort, but the rewards are immense as is the relief. It is essential that you find your own way, your own inner guidance, and connection. Without that, you will blow in the wind of everyone else's views.

If someone has hurt you, ask yourself 'What part of me is wounded?' Is it your ego, the aspect of you that is sensitive to criticism because of low self-worth and always needs to be right? Or perhaps it's the part of you that wants to keep the peace, keep everyone happy, be friends with everyone? Or does it not matter what the other person thinks or does?

If things aren't done the way you want, if there is an attempt to control another and a desire in a situation for the outcome you desire, that is what causes the problem. Let that go, and you are another step closer to the freedom you are seeking.

Don't get pulled into the dramas of others, and don't let others fuel you into making your own. The more we judge others, the more we feed the drama. The more we allow the judgement of others to affect us, the more we are going to get lost in the dead end of trying to please others.

If you truly want a peaceful life, then evaluating others and finding them wanting has to stop. Step back, take a breath, and allow others to be who they are and make their own choices. That is what we want for ourselves, and that is what others want from us. Make it a daily practice to observe yourself, catch any judgements of others, and allow people to be.

In the next chapter, we will look at ways to resolve these core issues at their root. For now, become aware of what is happening, what you do to avoid getting hurt, to keep the peace and whether it really is keeping the peace, or holding you back from who you are.

Keep a note in your journal of what you observe.

How to Forgive and Get Yourself Unstuck

Whether recent, or whether you are sometime down the line from the divorce, it is likely you have asked yourself, will I ever be able to forgive fully and if so how long will it take? Unsurprisingly, research has shown that where there is forgiveness, there is an improvement in life satisfaction, which underscores the importance of taking this topic seriously.

Let's start by looking at the facts. Horrible things have happened. Horrible things have been said. Horrible actions have been taken.

You know you can't change the past. Neither do you want to keep bringing all your history with you. But the past keeps rearing its head. The feelings continue to come up along with the anger, the frustration, the guilt, etc.

Now, what to do?

Begin at the beginning.

Why Is Forgiveness So Difficult?

When we haven't forgiven someone, every time we think about them or a situation they were involved in, we have an emotional reaction, and uncomfortable and painful feelings arise. Then our mind can kick into gear and start to go over the situation; the feelings intensify as we remember more. We analyse, re-run it, resulting in more emotions, more thoughts, even more opinions and the whole thing escalates. At some point, we may realise what we are doing and say to our mind to stop. We might try to distract ourselves, to prevent the whole scenario growing again. If we push it away, but we haven't resolved the pattern, it will sit there until another trigger sets it off again. In other words, lack of forgiveness destroys your peace.

The same can happen in conversations. We rerun the same situation repeatedly. We air our feelings; we express our thoughts, they both grow as we feed them with our attention. Others may help us with their contributions. There's no resolution. We might temporarily feel better for attributing blame, but afterwards nothing in the situation has changed, except we've expanded, grown, and refreshed the feelings and thoughts that ultimately only cause us pain.

Someone once had an entire conversation with me, and I didn't say a single word. This person spoke for himself and then for me, then responded as himself and so on, for several times until he had come to a conclusion that made him as mad as a wasp for reactions to which I had not contributed. I merely watched the scenario taking place. It was quite eye-opening to observe. He was so confident of my stance there was no point saying anything, even if I'd been able to squeeze in a word or two. It showed me precisely what we do in our heads when we run and re-run conversations and end up feeling angry or drained.

Some people react to painful situations by pushing the whole thing under the carpet and refusing to speak about it. They hope it will go away and that by giving it no external energy, by entirely avoiding the painful feelings as much as possible, they will be able to carry on with their lives beyond it. But harbouring the grudge or burying the feelings means not addressing them, which in turn means energy is being used to hold them there. There is a sense of being stuck.

And the very fact that energy is being used to keep feelings in place means there will be tension and stress, which can lead to illness.

What Can You Do?

Your aim is to be free. You want to live a life unencumbered by the events of the past and to live joyfully in the present moment. Resentment towards another is like carrying a huge weight around. It's taking precious energy and precious time. It's critical for your health and well being, as well as your ability to move on in life and create what you want, that you find a way to drop it, and drop it fast!

Tough Love Alert!

Forgiveness Exercise

The first step is to take a situation where you hurt another person. Sit quietly and imagine yourself as that person, get a sense of how they are feeling, what it is like being them. Really become them. When you have achieved this to the extent that it's possible, replay the scenario with you as if you are that other person, the person on the receiving end of you. Watch your face from their point of view, hear the words directed at you, observe how this makes you feel as if you are the other person.

What's it like to be on the receiving end of you?

You may well experience feelings of sadness and grief. Allow all the emotions to come to the surface, feel them entirely, and allow them to move through you.

Accept that you acted out of unawareness. If you find yourself feeling bad, you have gone into self-judgement. Pull back from judgement, and assure yourself that it's ok to feel the grief and sadness because you want to heal and move forward with compassion. Your purpose here is to forgive yourself.

For completeness, now look at any other situations in your life that may need this attention. If things pop into your head later, know that you can return to this exercise and repeat the procedure to reach the place of self-forgiveness.

The next step is to take a situation where you were the recipient of another's lack of awareness. Go into that scene and watch it. Your mind will now see that they too were acting out of non-love and didn't know any better. You will be aware that they are no different to you. Just as you felt compassion for yourself, you will have access to find compassion for them. This compassion is your route to forgiveness. Compassion is forgiveness.

When you see another as yourself, when you know that you were both acting from ignorance and you have fully felt all the feelings that come up, compassion remains.

Again, this is not to condone bad behaviour. When you see and accept it is from ignorance, there is a shift. You can walk away with no weight, no burden to hold you back. As we keep saying, you cannot change another, but instead, you have made an enormous shift within yourself, and that is where the important stuff happens. It will set you free and as a consequence change your life and your perspective. It is also possible that old pains and niggles may fade away. Amazing.

We've looked at some tough stuff. We've dug deep into motivations, new understandings, and how to reduce and deal with the negative emotional impact of your changing circumstances, so you can set yourself emotionally free and move on. Now let's change it up, and look at the more immediate upsides.

The Benefits: Have a Look at the Good Stuff!

When one door of happiness closes, another opens; but often we look so long at the closed door that we do not see the one which has been opened for us.
– Helen Keller

What are the benefits of your situation?

I bet many of you at first will say not much! But I am also willing to bet that there are things that you can do now that you couldn't do before. When you can begin to see that the change of circumstance isn't all bad, you will also be aware of some advantages. I would encourage you to take a good look at your life now and see what you have gained following your breakup.

It might be that you no longer have to walk on eggshells to keep the peace.

You might realise you can now set your routine, your own timetable. You can go to bed when you want, get up when you want, eat what you want.

You might find your sleep time is not interrupted by snoring or a late-night arrival.

It might be that you have a more open and honest life now, that you no longer feel you have to hide difficult situations or betrayals.

You might find some relief in not having to deal with another's moods and demands.

For myself, it took me a while to see this positive side of the breakup, but it was transformational when I grasped it.

The first time our children went away on holiday with my ex and his new partner, I was devastated. I moped about and couldn't concentrate on anything for feeling left out and abandoned while they were off having fun. I was their mother, and I wasn't involved. I felt excluded from my own family's life.

On day four, I woke up and realised what I was doing. I had a week to myself, with no distractions, to do what I wanted without the demands of young children. I'd wasted three days pining, and I wasn't going to lose anymore. Instead of living with regrets for the way things were, I accepted the situation, which allowed me to move on. After that, I used the time the children were away to accomplish what I wanted, things I would never have been able to realise had I still been married and working full time with a young family. I trained in various therapies and, in short, set myself up with the skills I needed to leave my office job and move on to a life that was more aligned with who I was.

The Power of Appreciation

Appreciation for what you already have is critical to creating the life you want. We will talk more about this in Chapter 5, but, for now, I want you to be aware of the importance of seeing the benefits and having gratitude for what you do have in your life already. For those of us living in western society, there's so much we can take for granted, such as running water, a flushing toilet, a roof over our head, food on the table, friends, travel mobility, the ability to make free choices, freedom of speech, etc. Simply by feeling into the positives that you do have in your life, you're a step closer to the life you want. That's the power of appreciation.

It's a fact of life backed up by universal law, if you're a glass half empty as opposed to half full sort of person then sadly that's the life you will get. If you want your life to be not only a half full but a 100% full, then truly feeling appreciation for what you have is a great place to start.

Try writing a list of everything you can be grateful for, and all the things you appreciate every night before sleeping. Don't stop until you have over 100 items on your list. Falling asleep from a place full of gratitude and appreciation is a great way to set up your next day to be a fulfilling one.

A Tool for Healthy Decision-making: The Two Paths

When a long-term relationship comes to an end, it is rarely a clean break. There has been so much emotional investment, that for each party to simply part and immediately start afresh is almost impossible. For most of us, at some point, the uncoupling is a messy process. The end is therefore often characterised by a lot of to-ing and fro-ing, asking questions, and trying to find the best way forward. Sometimes sentimentality has the upper hand, other times the head takes over.

It is draining and disruptive. One minute everything is going one way, the next it's going another. One minute you feel one option is the right decision, the next it's something else.

Jeanette's husband of 14 years had walked out a year ago to live with someone who he had been having an affair with. Jeanette has been working hard to re-establish a life for herself and her children, to build up an income to support herself, and develop good working relationships and a group of friends.

Now, her husband was back in touch and wanted them to give their marriage another go. When she saw him again Jeanette was confused by the emotional feelings she still had for him and wasn't sure what she wanted and what to do anymore.

To help with this sort of dilemma, you can sit quietly, breathe deeply into your belly a few times and relax. Then visualise ahead of you two paths. Choose one of your options. What is the feeling as you envision this path? Go into the detail and sense everything you can about it. Feel it from every angle, the pluses, and the minuses. Remember, the key here is truly feeling what it would be like to live this life.

After this, come back to the starting point again, look at the two paths, and, this time, choose the second one. Feel how your life will be if you take this path, the options open to you, and how your life can be.

In our example, Jeanette could look at where her life would go and how it would be if she and her husband got back together. She could look at what she would need to do if she took that path and what it would be like to be with him again. What questions would arise? Would she be able to trust him not to disrupt her life again, and, if not, what would that feel like to live with that on a daily basis? Would he be able to accommodate the person she had become now that she had started a new life journey without him? She could ponder whether she felt he had her best interests at heart and whether he is looking at how he can work out the problems that led to him leaving for another in the first place.

Then Jeanette could look at the second path, the one where she builds upon what she has started for herself, the path that would carry on and expand from what she has already created for herself over the last 12 months or so. As she feels deeply into both ways, she will be clearer on the implications of both and be able to get in touch with which is going to serve her best and which one feels the right path for her.

When you have a dilemma and can genuinely feel what life is like for yourself down each of the paths open to you, you will have your answer as to which one you will want to choose.

This exercise is also useful to help you see where you are going in life generally and help motivate you to make the changes to get where you want to be. Feel into the path where you realise your dreams and do all the things you'd like to do. Then feel into life continuing on the way you are going now. If there's a stark contrast, you will know that it is only the need to take action that is stopping you from having the life you want.

Taking Action Will Change Your Life

When you take steps to implement your new understandings, you start to move and your life can start to change very fast.

Excitement grows about what you're discovering and can apply to your life. Your life becomes steadier and more aligned with who you genuinely are. You become more precise about your life purpose. You will also realise that life can be so much more than you previously thought. It also encourages you to move on and leave the past where it belongs.

Now all these things may make sense. Indeed, you may have heard about or tried to implement many of them before, but that doesn't always help you put it into practice, and this is the key to sustainable changes that get you where you want to be. We don't necessarily do what we know is best for us. It's very confusing. Why is that?

In the next chapter, we will look at what is stopping you from actually doing what you know in your heart to be in your best interest.

Summary

- Accept life is going to be different so you might as well embrace it.
- The only person you can change is you.
- Become whole in your own right, and you will attract another who is also whole.
- Step out of the victim/rescuer/persecutor cycle.
- Let go of guilt, self-blame, and regrets.
- Express your feelings; don't bottle them up.

- Drop all the judgements and opinions of others.
- Forgive yourself and others.
- See the opportunity you have been given and the benefits of your new situation.
- You can choose your path.

Main Action Steps

1. Dealing with grief and loss.
2. Noting in your journal your new understandings.
3. The forgiveness exercise.
4. The two paths exercise.

The Result

You experience peace.

CHAPTER FOUR

The Third Key: Rooting Out the Cause of Your Problems

We don't see things as they are, we see them as we are.
– Anaïs Nin

If you can find and eliminate the cause of your problems, this will bring you freedom. Therefore, it's worth asking yourself why you are in the situation you find yourself in the first place.

In previous chapters, we've looked at how you can view things differently, understand yourself and your situation more, and make changes where needed. As a result, your confidence and self-worth improve, leading to greater clarity and the ability to move on.

You might be wondering why did you not know some of this before. Why did you have to muddle along in this thing called life and have a crisis before you could find these things out? When we are born, we are not given a roadmap.

In this chapter, we are going to look at why some or all of this is new to you and how come you didn't know these things. Why weren't you taught this at school? What is it that makes life so difficult to navigate, full of bloopers and errors, and all sorts of hard to handle situations?

Here in the UK, there was a situation comedy called 'dinnerladies' set in an office canteen. At the end of the final series, after twists and turns, ups and downs, two of the leading characters eventually get together as a couple. 'Will we live happily ever after?' asks one. 'No,' says the other, 'I reckon we'll just blunder about, messing it up like everyone else.' The live audience roars with laughter at this raw truth after the romantic build up.

Our expectations, especially in a story, are the 'happily ever after', but the reality is so often very different. We may have dreams, but we also know that they can shatter. The problem is, we don't really understand why. We blame ourselves, we blame others, but that doesn't really help. Why do we self-sabotage then? Why do others never do what we think would have avoided the issue?

I hear people ask, 'Why me?' about their breakup. 'What did I do wrong? Did I really deserve this?'

As well as not knowing why life guidance wasn't available to us before or at a younger age, we may also be wondering why we keep doing the same things over and over, even though we know better and can see that it's not serving us. Maybe we wonder why the same things keep happening to us. By now, you may even be asking yourself what is really going on. Why am I not getting where I want to be?

We strive for the external to make us happy, but it doesn't. We try to change, to let go, to move on, but we only have partial success. The whole thing can get incredibly frustrating.

We can understand where things could be better; it can all make perfectly logical sense, and we can look to see where we can change this or that. The problem is that knowing and understanding it doesn't always help us to actually make the changes we need to. Or, if we do make changes, it can be hard to be consistent and keep up the momentum.

My breakup happened suddenly and unexpectedly, and I was utterly and most definitely unprepared for it. Over time, as I began to put the ideas and concepts in the previous chapters into practice, my life got better, but then something would always happen, and it would get worse again. My world would be rocked anew. There would be a parenting issue or an event arrangement problem or even just a total misunderstanding that would set off a whole series of events. There were times when I felt I couldn't do right for doing wrong. No matter how many self-help books I read, no matter how many therapies I trained in, no matter how hard I tried to put it all into practice, I was still being buffeted around.

This cycle went on for several years until I was shown some more profound truths that I had been entirely unaware of. What I have learnt since then has been nothing short of life transforming. Until then, I had no idea that I only had half the picture, half the answers I was seeking.

When you commit to getting to the cause of why your life has been the way it is, it is a revelation. Pieces of the jigsaw start to fall into place and mysteries solved. You understand yourself more, and, as a consequence, you understand others more. Life is less random.

Yes, there are challenges. Of course, this is true, but you will have an anchor to rely on, resources to draw on to help you through, and you can see a bigger picture than you ever thought possible. You realise that life is so much more than you ever imagined, and it's beautiful.

Without this step, you can develop coping mechanisms, you can get to a place where things are generally OK. But there will always be the feeling that things could change in a flash and leave you floundering again.

If you are ready to go deeper, to understand yourself and therefore the world and others more, if you are prepared for all the incredible rewards this brings, then I am genuinely excited to share this with you.

Understanding Why We Do What We Do

When a baby is born, it is like a sponge. It has no language, but it does have feelings and the ability to make sounds. These two traits mean a baby can make its needs known, as any new parent will verify. As a child grows, the sponge keeps absorbing information from the new world it finds itself in.

We are not born with a guidebook, but we do have parents and caregivers who aim to show us the way. The big question is do those people really understand life themselves, or are they continuing to pass on what they learnt from their parents and caregivers and so on?

For example, what is considered to be normal in one family is seen as rude in another.

In Jemima's family, everyone helped themselves to what they wanted from the fruit bowl. If you wanted a grape, you merely plucked one from the bunch and popped it in your mouth.

When Jemima first went to her husband's family home and did the same, she got disapproving looks. She then noticed a pair of scissors by the bowl and watched what other family members did. In this household, there was an expectation that you neatly cut the exact number of grapes you wanted to eat from the bunch.

You may think this is a silly and trivial example, but it was enough to make Jemima uncomfortable. She was not meeting expectations, even though she had no idea beforehand what those expectations were. The grape-eating rules in her family were entirely different from her husband's family. Both families thought their way was right and that if people behaved differently, they were wrong, or at least, out of step.

If there can be conflict at the level of grape eating, it is not surprising that we find it so hard to navigate our way through life and relationships. Where does this all start?

We Have All Been Conditioned

Everyone loves babies and young ones, don't they? They can melt even the hardest of hearts with their endearing openness and innocence. The observation 'out of the mouth of babes…' conveys how they can express simple wisdom with purity. They are connected to their limitless, unconditioned self and are not afraid to show it.

When children grow, this openness changes, as they are taught the ways of the world, or should I say their world, the world into which they have been born. We have all been through this process one way or another. We have all been conditioned to behave in a way that is expected by our society, family, town, school, college, and community by telling us we are good if we conform, and we are bad if we don't. On the whole, we tended to accept this because we came to believe that others knew better than us, because they were older, more experienced, or had some sort of authority over us. Or we might have rebelled, and, as they say, thrown the baby out with the bathwater and rejected everything without censor. Whatever your reaction, the result was you learnt to distrust your own inner guidance.

What this conditioning has done is separate us from our true self. The open and joyful young child we once were has become something different to either fit in or to rebel. The child forgets that they could both experience and express life sourced from their feelings as they did as infants. Instead, the child learns to live a limited life, either following or fighting the rules and seeks external validation instead of drawing on wisdom from within.

This switch from reliance on internal guidance to external guidance and its consequent suppression of the true self is a significant cause of mental illness and depression. It's the reason those coming out of a relationship breakup ask, 'Who am I?' and question their own identity and sometimes their sanity. Given the conditioning we have been fed, it is apparent that slipping into steadily limiting ourselves in both subtle and less subtle ways within the relationship is easily done. There is a tendency to conform to what we think will bring the 'happily ever after'.

A UK TV documentary in the 1960s showed children aged 7 years from widely varying backgrounds talking about their lives and their dreams for the future. The programme concept was based on the Jesuit premise 'give me a child until aged seven, and I will give you the man'. The TV production team then decided to revisit the children every seven years to see how their lives were panning out and if they had gone in foreseeable directions.

As you might suppose, generally, children with lower expectations in life at seven fulfilled just that, and, those with bigger ambitions as a result of a broader, more affluent, start in life, expanded more.

It was particularly poignant when a lost, low, and severely depressed 30 something was shown the film of himself as a bright 7-year-old. Shocked to see himself as he was at that age, he wistfully comments that he could not remember ever having been that happy. That was how separated from his limitless, unconditioned self he had become. Interestingly, in later episodes, he was shown as having turned his life around. Maybe seeing himself at that young age woke something up in him and gave him hope?

Conditioning is what you've been taught as right by society and those you believe to be in authority over you or who you consider know better than you. This conditioning tells you what to expect from your life and how it should be; it declares to you what is right and wrong. That declaration is then accepted as absolute because you believe the person who is telling you knows best. We have all been exposed to this.

However, we know from the grape eating example that conditioning is not an absolute truth. It is something generally accepted by a group or individual, but it comes from the external interpreted experience, not from internal guidance.

And you likely know from your own evidence that the happily ever after you had hoped for or expected hasn't happened.

A baby uses its feelings to navigate its world and make its needs known. As it grows, and especially when it's taught language, it is conditioned to behave appropriately for the world it is living in.

Often, formational experiences are from painful or stressful situations.

Aged 5, Sandra was playing in the garden with her younger sister Anne, 3. Sandra had just started school, was enjoying the new play equipment they had in the gym and had discovered she loved climbing and swinging on the ropes. Excited by her new skills, she decided to scale one of the trees in the garden. Anne wanted to join the game too, so Sandra helped her up. But Anne fell and cut her head and started screaming.

Their mother rushed out and angrily shouted at Sandra for not taking better care of her younger sister and letting her do things beyond her capabilities. Already upset by her sister's accident, Sandra was further traumatised by her mother's reaction and was shocked to have gone suddenly from a joyful time playing with her sister to being in trouble. Sandra previously had no idea that she had been doing anything wrong. She felt sick and was shaking while her sister was receiving all the attention for her cut.

The impact of this shock reverberated throughout Sandra's childhood. She was, after that, always very cautious in her play, wary of hurting anyone, and of making another mistake that could lead to more blame, and therefore pain, by being at the receiving end of her sharp-tongued mother or indeed anyone else in authority for that matter.

This pattern unconsciously continued to play out throughout Sandra's life. Always cautious, always looking for the safe option, keeping a wary eye out for anything she may have missed, she was always trying to be ahead of any situation in order never to be wrong-footed again.

This experience for Sandra is an example of what Mike Robinson, in his book The True Dynamics of Life, calls the first point of pain. It is the stopping point in a child's life when they first experience fear arising from an act of non-love from another, something that typically happens before the age of seven.

How the child reacts at this point is pivotal to how they deal with pain or fear for the rest of their life unless they release it. If not, the emotion becomes stuck, the connection with the inner voice or guidance is lost, and the duality between trying to minimise or avoid pain and seeking pleasure has begun.

This duality also involves a division inside. A split occurs between the male and female aspects of the child (regardless of physical gender), whereby the female element is seen as weak by the male element, and the male is distrusted by the female. No longer whole, and because the inner guidance has been shut down, life is now lived from this place of both duality and attempts to protect the self. The first point of pain is the origin of why we believe we are separate from one another. It is also the reason there are so many children in adults bodies.

Conditioning then is the belief that you have taken on as true and the belief upon which you take action. It comes both from personally dramatic situations as Sandra experienced, and it can also be subtler, like the ideas and behaviour of your family that you accept as normal and absorb and which become part of yourself. Conditioning is passed down the generations as the truth and taken on board at the expense of your intuition, dreams, and hopes. If no one questions their conditioned beliefs, it is no wonder nothing much is changing in the world concerning relationships. It is no surprise the same mistakes and scenarios are continually being repeated both in history and our lives, and is the reason we are not taught effective and practical skills to deal with life when attending school.

When your conditioning is present, it is not possible to hear the message from your inner self, from your inner guidance.

Conditioning is the veil through which you see the world. It's the reaction you keep repeating from your subconscious to keep you safe and in the known and which acts as a barrier between your true inner self and the physical life you live in the world. It means patterns continue to repeat, and you don't always know why; they seem to bubble up of their own accord.

If you find yourself reacting automatically with anger, frustration, sarcasm, or cynicism for example, then you know you have responded from your conditioning. If you can pause, see what is being shown to you, as well as give yourself some space to feel for the response, then you know you are moving on.

It is because we have lost that inner connection that we don't know who we are anymore. While things are trundling along, while life is routine and predictable, you may not notice it. When a crisis like a divorce happens, when your world is turned upside down, and the framework within which you expected to spend the rest of your life has crumbled, big questions loom large. Who am I and how did my life end up here? There is a deep sense of loneliness. You may be able to see now that this loneliness stems from the fundamental separation between your inner knowing, your limitless self if you like, and from the limited physical self, which is acting from a position of conditioning. Our unconditioned, limitless self is the connection to the whole that we seek, but when we are only in the grip of our conditioned self, it is impossible to access.

Conditioning means you are unable to live connected to who you truly are, to be spontaneously in the moment. Instead, you are living from what you have learnt in the past, from situations and experiences, from memory, if you like. One client told me she wanted to escape from the living prison she felt she was in, this disconnection, this place of isolation.

Here is the first tool for moving beyond conditioning.

Living in the Present

When I first was told that my marriage was in deep trouble and that I could not do anything about it, I went into shock. I retched with it. My mind and my conditioning also went into overdrive in an attempt to protect me. I felt I was a bad person and it had to be my fault. My mind kept going over and over the situation trying to find a solution, but of course, getting nowhere except for making me more and more miserable. I couldn't sleep, and yet the only place I wanted to be was under the covers pretending this wasn't happening and hoping to wake up from the nightmare. I was panicking about the future and how I would cope, and I desperately did not want to be a divorcee or for my children to experience the breakup of their parents' marriage.

I was advised to take everything minute by minute. I can see now what good advice this was, but, frankly, I had never tried to do this before, and I found it alien and initially virtually impossible. I had always used language and logic to resolve any issues, so to let go and live in the moment was a herculean task. I knew I had to do it, however, because I'd had enough of the alternative, which led me nowhere. I gave it my best shot, and gradually I began to dig myself out of my self-inflicted hole.

I now know that every time I use the external beliefs and authority to guide me rather than listening to my instinctive feelings, I am moving further away from being in touch with my intuition, my limitless self. The more I listen to and act on my feelings and intuition, the more my life flows and expands to the life I want.

This intuition is there on a minute by minute basis; it is in the present. If my mind wanders to the future or starts chewing over the past–again–I am unable to feel for the present moment guidance.

The only time we have to live is in the present. The future and the past do not exist. The past is known, the future never happens. The present is unknown; it is the adventure of life.

The mind wants to resolve issues by referring to the past, but that is not its role. We can work towards a future that we want, but we will only create it by focusing on the now, the actions we can take in this moment, and then in this moment and then again in this moment. If we think we will be happy in the future when something else materialises, when the stars align, then it's not going to happen. We create our happiness now.

Living in the present, taking action in the present, is the only place we can truly live.

Before my divorce, I was utterly ignorant of this way of being and was living primarily by trying to keep everything under tight control to keep myself safe. And you have seen where that got me. In a right pickle.

As I kept on searching for the truth of why things were the way they were, I began to understand the impact my childhood conditioning had had on my life, and I started to clear away old patterns leaving space for new.

There was and is no blame on my parents and everyone who was trying to look out for me. I know they were and are doing their best, and I truly value the input everyone has had on my life. What I had to do is learn how to hold onto my true self in the face of others acting from their conditioning.

It is a challenge to master being in the present moment at all times. My mind loves to try to tell me that it isn't a safe place to be, that I need to work things out logically using information from the past. The mind is excellent at solving puzzles and loves to do that. You need your mind to tell you how to drive your car, what roads to take to get to where you want to be, and how to lock it when you park it etc. But if the mind is given free rein and allowed to run amok, you will find yourself going over and over the same scenario and getting similar results. You can even actually end up feeling worse. When this happens, you know you have gone from working on a present moment issue to be resolved, to thinking about the past or future. It is stressful, creates tension in the body and will eventually lead to ill health. For these reasons alone, it is worth mastering living in the present.

The solution is in the present. Living is in the present.

Here is an exercise that can help you with that.

Sit quietly and bring your focus to your abdomen, just below the navel. Breathe deeply into this area through the nose. Feel your belly start to swell. Exhale through the mouth, slowly and thoroughly. Repeat, keeping your focus on your breathing and abdomen. If your mind starts to wander, gently bring your attention back to the breath.

Spend some time each morning and evening doing this. You can use this exercise if you are feeling stressed or if you have trouble quieting the mind and sleeping.

Question Everything

Now you have seen that you and very nearly everyone who has ever lived on this planet has been conditioned. We have also talked about how the only place to live is in the present moment. As a result, you may be starting to look at the world and your part in it a little differently. That's great. You are on the move.

There is a constant running through your life relating to your beliefs and outlook. Observe everything in your life, and you will see it. To do this, start to look at your habits and patterns, such as how you eat, what you eat, how you organise your day, and how you speak. Are you different depending on who you talk to etc.? You will begin to see how the unconscious conditioned part of yourself is playing out. This is the aspect of you that is beyond the conscious and the known. When you look at this conditioned part and start to let it go, as you turn more to the present and the intuitive, your life will begin to flow more.

The conditioned part of your subconscious is the barrier between you and your limitless self. As you begin to bring down that barrier, the one that society has placed in you and that you accepted, as you chip away at it, poke holes in it, and undermine it, you have increasing access to this limitless self that has been waiting patiently for your reconnection with it.

Colleen was having problems maintaining her decision to leave an abusive relationship. She felt guilty. She looked at her habits of needing to please people, of putting others needs first, of trying to make everything alright for others and her fear of standing up for herself. Colleen then traced the patterns back to several painful events in her childhood that had moulded her behaviour and her subsequent reactions when in challenging situations.

She saw that she needed to put herself and her own needs first rather than scattering herself thinly, as she tried to dance to everyone else's tune. She was then able to see precisely why her current behaviour was causing so many problems, both for herself and others.

As Colleen delved deep into self-care, she found she had a clearer understanding of the bigger picture and her role in situations. She was no longer caught up in the details and could catch manipulative behaviour from her husband and others quicker and quicker. Seeing it for what it is, and with no blame or judgement, she could respond differently and in a way that also took into account her needs and dreams for her own life.

Colleen is now a strong, centred woman, living a life she once thought beyond her reach. As well as finding new strength, she has retained and continues to develop her big heart, soft femininity, and creativity. In other words, she has become whole.

See Others as Your Mirror

Your limitless self is the part of you that is intuitive and has always been there, overseeing the bigger picture of your life. It is trying to help you to go beyond your conditioned and limited self. It does this by bringing to you the very situations that will best show you what you are doing that takes you out of alignment with your true self. When you see and understand this, you can then change it for something more aligned to who you truly are, which means you are one more step closer to the life you want. In other words, if you understand what you are being shown and take action to change yourself, then you no longer need that experience and can now leave it behind.

However, like me, it is highly unlikely you were ever told about this process and how it works and are therefore more likely to see the experience as negative, something to be borne, rejected, fought against or avoided at all costs.

I had a troublesome relationship with my mother throughout our life together. I now know she was an excellent teacher for me, and I have since made peace with her and thanked her profoundly for showing me so many important aspects in my life that needed attention. At the time, however, I saw her role in my life as pretty much entirely negative.

When she died, while I was sad to lose the idea of having a mother, I was also relieved not to be faced with the challenges she regularly brought to me. But something bizarre happened to make my relief very short-lived. A relationship I was in at the time seamlessly took over the challenging behaviour I had experienced from my mother. It was quite remarkable and so spectacularly evident to me what was happening that I woke up to it and started to look at the situation differently.

I realised that there was something I needed to address. I started to look in the mirror and see what this situation was showing me. I'll admit there was a myriad of things, but the main ones were that I needed to stand on my own two feet and not avoid conflict. I needed to resolve issues from a place of peace, not from a reaction of anger. I needed to allow other people to be who they were, do what they wanted to do, and not try to change them. As I began to learn how to do this, the situation changed. It was a big learning curve for me, and it took a while. I didn't have the deeper understanding that I now have and have been able to share with you in this book. At that time, I did a lot of it from trial and error.

Fast forward a couple of decades, and I came to realise that my mother and I were, and are, not separate. That her behaviour towards me was from ignorance, from her own conditioning, fear, and lack of self-worth. I can see now that, in my interactions with her, I was acting from my own lack of understanding and self-worth. No wonder our relationship was fraught; we were mirroring each other perfectly.

Each person, each situation in your life, is there to show you another aspect of yourself. When you understand that aspect of yourself, when you release its power over you and let the unknown come in that bit further to guide you minute by minute, the situation resolves itself. Sometimes a little repeating test will come in just to be sure you've really got it. If you have, it will move away because it isn't part of you or your world anymore. And what is left is love.

For Colleen, whose story I told you earlier, this means she will not be going into an abusive relationship again. She knows her true worth and honours that daily, so she does not need to seek her worth from others who can't give it to her.

When you first take a good look in the mirror provided by another and see yourself, it can be pretty uncomfortable. Know you are being shown your limited, conditioned self, the very thing that is acting as a barrier between you and your limitless, unconditioned self. When you see yourself in that mirror, you have a choice. You can accept what is being shown to you, give thanks for the understanding, and change your reaction and behaviour accordingly. Or you can deny the lesson and carry on. In which case, the experience will continue coming to you in different formats until you do learn from the experience. Or not.

Not looking in the mirror and seeing a situation as yours to deal with is the very reason why people repeat the same scenarios over and over again. It's why people find they cannot move on and have the relationship they really want. The universe is very logical. Until the experience is understood, the next step cannot be taken.

Every situation you grow from brings you closer and closer to alignment with your unconditioned limitless self, the true you. The more aligned you are, the more likely you are to attract others who are also similarly placed. It is a universal law that like attracts like. When you look in the mirror and make the changes, you are going to be drawing to you people who reflect you, and the more you yourself are someone you genuinely love and fully accept, the happier and more fulfilled those relationships will be.

Clearing the Patterns that are Keeping You Stuck

We spoke about physically decluttering your environment in Chapter Two. Just as physically decluttering provides space for new and makes you feel heaps better in the process, so clearing your conditioning gives you space to create the life you want. We are going to be looking at how you can develop your vision in the next chapter, so to make sure you are in an excellent place to do just that, here are a few techniques to help move out the old and make space for the new.

1. Fast writing–write everything down that is bothering you. Don't stop until you feel you have written everything you can. Don't worry about grammar or if it is

legible; just write it all out as fast as you can. Don't reread it (i.e. don't put it all back in again!) When you have finished, tear it up, shred it, or burn it.

2. Microphone–take yourself to a quiet and private place and imagine you have a microphone in your hand. Start speaking about everything you are feeling, all that is frustrating you, everyone who is annoying you, anything that has happened that is still bothering you or whatever it is that is causing your mind to be working overtime. You will feel that, once you have started, it is easy to keep going until things quieten down, and you have a sense of release and peace. If not, then keep going.

3. Letter writing–if you have an issue with someone, a parent, family member, a peer, someone from your past or someone in your life now that is affecting your peace, write them a letter setting out everything you want to say to them. You may find it is full of expletives and anger. Don't reread it. When you have finished, burn or shred it, and if that is the end of it that's fine. You could then, however, want to write a second, more factual, letter that you may now feel is the one you want to send, one that expresses your true self and feelings about what happened.

By clearing the conditioning, you are making room for a new way of being. When this new way of being starts to take hold, you are forming a solid foundation from where you can build a life of your choosing. This new foundation sets the stage for the emotional freedom that moving past the pain of your divorce is going to give you. Instead of a life set up to please others and fit in, it will be one that sings to your heart and from which you can express your full potential.

In the next chapter, we are going to look at exactly how you can do just that by creating the life you want.

Summary

- The cause of why you are where you are is your conditioning.
- Conditioning is the veil through which we see and react in the world.
- Everyone has experienced this because it is passed through the generations as truth.
- The first point of pain from before aged 7 years old sets up a pattern of how we react from then on.
- When you see that these patterns have been ruling your life and you take steps to change this, you are making space for an entirely new way of being.

Main Action Steps

1. Focus on living in the present.
2. Use the mindful breathing exercise.
3. See where you are conditioned – question everything.
4. See others as your mirror.
5. Utilise the clearing techniques:
    - fast writing
    - microphone technique
    - letter writing

The Result

You are on the road to freedom.

CHAPTER FIVE

The Fourth Key: Develop A Vision for The Future

Today spend a moment, just a moment for you, no excuses, and melt into the feeling of what it would be like for you to be free, to express your greatest talents, gifts and dreams. Once you have this, don't move from this feeling. Don't let anyone slam you down into that pit of worthlessness, that pit that tells you that you can't.

Do this, hold it moment-to-moment, every day, and physical life will follow the direction of that thought and feeling of freedom.

The only tools you have within to navigate this life are thoughts and feelings. The only tools you have externally to navigate this life are your actions and your voice. Own them all. Master them by directing them and create the life that you were born to live.
– Jo Le-Rose

Your Vision for Your Life and Your Joy

As you develop self-love through self-care and after all the hard work of looking at things anew, decluttering outside and in, as well as addressing that pesky conditioning, you can then enjoy having fun deciding where you want your life to go.

When you start to see beyond the pain, the hurt, and the drama, you can get excited about the opportunities you are being given to go and do what you want, to do what makes your heart sing, and try out new things.

In this chapter, we are going to bring together what you've read, so you can take action to create your future.

One final thing before we get started.

I want you to know that you are safe. You have been discovering your inner power, the very life in you, the intelligence and intuition in you, and this will show you how to open up to your new life, how to blossom and flourish. The false security is in the conditioned part of you that tries to keep you safe but whose vision is limited to the valley bottom, to the detail. Your limitless self, the unconditioned you is flying high in the sky seeing everything and is there to guide you as you go.

So, let's tap into that high-flying guidance and get going.

How We Create

For your creation to be optimally successful, you need to know and understand the tools with which you create.

Thoughts

The law of attraction says whatever we think about we create. If you are thinking judgemental, negative thoughts, then that is what will come to you. If your thoughts are full of appreciation for what you do have, then you will have more of that. It is that simple.

I know. Easy to say, not so easy to do. But with your new awareness, you will be able to change this moment by moment. If you slip up, don't worry about creating negativity; drop it and move on. You don't want to compound it. Draw on your new understanding that it is your conditioning that has been keeping you stuck in the negativity and that you don't live in that place anymore.

You can probably now see how important it is to do the work and exercises in the previous sections in order to bring into your life what you want.

Words

What we say has an energy behind it. There is an intent that comes with words that the actual words themselves may belie. We have all been lied to, and you know what it feels like when the words and truth don't align. Keep your words aligned with honesty, and you will see changes.

If you don't have anything to say, don't speak. If your words are judgemental, then they say more about you than the person you are judging and as such will keep you from moving forward. If you are saying what you think other people want to hear rather than what you feel inside, be aware that you are slipping into people-pleasing mode, which has its pitfalls.

On the other hand, if your words come from a place of genuine love and desire to uplift others and move yourself and others forward, then that is what will come back to you.

Actions

Everything begins with a thought, but it is actions that see it through.

Bethany had been living in the family home since her ex left three years before. He now wanted his share of the equity in the house, as he was planning to get remarried. Bethany had young children and told him she didn't want to disrupt their schooling by moving to a smaller home in a cheaper area.

Bethany realised she had made an assumption that she would not be able to get a house to meet her and the children's needs in the same area, so she decided to speak to the agents and see what was available. In other words, she challenged her closed negative thought and replaced it with a more open one that meant she could then follow through, take action, and speak different words than she had previously. Her thoughts had affected her words and consequently her actions.

Feelings

Now we come to the real powerhouse of creating what you want. Feelings are critical to whether you manifest successfully or not.

We have looked at how you can only change yourself, not another. If you want to be happy, for example, that is your responsibility; no one else can do it for you. You have the freedom to decide to be happy, or you can choose to stay in an unhappy place.

What that means is you have the choice to look at why you are unhappy and decide to take action needed to change that. It might be that you are being taken for granted or abused in some way. You can stay with the abuse or move on, as long as you are clear that the cause of your unhappiness lies within you and that you have the power to change it. As you accept this your approach will change, your inner strength grows, and the happy times will grow, too.

If thoughts come from an aligned place, then the actions, words, and feelings are more likely to be positive and aligned too, and the universe will respond by manifesting it for you. But if the emotions behind the thoughts, words, and actions are fear, doubt, worry, 'I can't have it', 'others can have it but not me', 'I'm not good enough,' etc. then the result is more of what you are feeling.

To continue using the story of Bethany above, if her thoughts about moving to a new house were fear-based ones, maybe stemming from a concern that she would lose out financially and not be able to survive if she did as her ex requested, and maybe from suspicion that he no longer had her best interests at heart, then the action and words will have fear in them too. The estate agent will likely consciously, or unconsciously, perceive that fear and respond according to his own conditioning. If he needs power over another to make him feel worthy, this could lead to him dismissing Bethany out of hand. If she goes in powerful and confident in herself, she is more likely to draw to her what she is looking for.

It is possible to start by creating what you want with positive thoughts, actions, words, and feelings, but if doubt or fear comes in then in effect you have told your subconscious self you want something different and put yourself back to square one. You then need to start building the positive momentum again.

As you master these tools of creation, you can begin to choose your life with confidence.

You've done all this fantastic preparation to understand why you are in the situation you are in and how you can change it. You know the tools of creation you need to utilise to bring into existence what you want. Now it's time to get started on making those dreams a reality!

Making What You Want a Reality

It might be that you are already very clear about what you want but are not sure about how to get things moving in the right direction to get there.

Alternatively, you might have loads of ideas about what you want to do but have difficulty narrowing it down to the ones you want to focus on. As a result, you may be finding your actions are scattered, and you feel frustrated that you can't seem to get where you want to be.

You may be someone who has had their dreams and ambitions so squashed over the years that you now feel out of touch with what you want, doubtful about what is possible and bereft of ideas.

Wherever you are now, in this chapter, we are going to look at ways you can get clarity on what you want and where you want to be. We will look at developing goals to aim for, and you can start to take consistently focused steps towards getting there.

I recommend you do this in two stages.

Step One

Start by making a list of all your basic needs such as a roof over your head, money to pay bills, eat well, and run a reliable car, etc.

Psychologically, once you know you have set out the basics you need in your life, you can let those go, knowing you have put that message out to yourself and the universe that you want your core needs to live on this planet to be covered. If you are in a situation where you have those basics covered already, give appreciation for them and for what they bring to your life, and move onto step two.

If you don't have these basics in place already, you will need to brainstorm how you are going to get them. You may need to utilise an existing skill to earn money to put them in place for example. Even if this work is not your dream life, look at it as providing for these essential basics while you set about putting things in place to move you on to your dreams. It is not the end goal; it is a means to an end, a stepping stone to the life you want. But whatever you do have, remember to give appreciation for it. Feel it fully. When we appreciate what we have in life, life brings us more of it. We are using feeling to create it.

Step Two

With the essentials covered one way or another, you are then free to allow yourself to dream and dream big about what you want in your life. This is where you get to do the really fun part, the part that lifts your heart and gives you immense joy!

Start to brainstorm everything you can think of, everything you want in your life, everything you love. Keep adding to it, take time to allow your desires to have full rein. You can mind map this by taking a large unlined piece of paper and putting in the middle of it something like 'my dream life'. Around this centre, add all the ideas you have for what you want in your life and how you want your life to be. Don't edit anything, keep the flow going. Don't be shy, don't limit yourself, get all your ideas out on paper, and see which ones you are connected to already and which ones you would like to link to more.

If you feel stuck, revisit your childhood and remember what your dreams for your future were then, what you loved to do, what gave you joy. It may bring up emotion to remember how you were then compared to how you are now. Allow this emotion to come up and be released and know that you are now able to reconnect to that lost part of you and bring it into your life.

Developing a vision board from all your ideas can be helpful. Search for pictures that convey what you are wanting. They can be literal pictures, or they can simply be pictures that evoke the feeling you are looking for.

Arrange these pictures on a board, and revisit it every day, twice a day, when you wake up and before you go to sleep. Take a few moments to look at your board and feel into the life it portrays to you, what it would be like to have what you are asking for, to live what you are setting out for yourself. For example, if you want a new house, look at your pictures, and feel what it would be like to live in that house, what each room would feel like, what the décor would feel like, what the view would feel like. Go into as much detail as you can.

Important Qualification

There is a significant qualification for everything we have spoken about in this chapter. Without it, you won't get the results you are looking for.

We have said how important feelings are to create what you want. There is one other requirement that you need to be aware of in order to forge the life you wish for successfully. To understand this, you need to be clear and honest with yourself about your own feelings and where they are taking you.

The nub of it is that there needs to be an element of service to others in your dreams.

The reason manifestation works in the way it does is the universe wants to expand and grow, and each of us plays a part in that. We are all in this together, which is why sages have been telling us for centuries that we are all one. The consciousness of humanity will grow as one. No one is getting ahead of the game, and no one will be left behind.

Given this understanding, if your dreams involve you wanting to have more than your fellow travellers in order for you to feel good about yourself and to feel safe or if your desires come from competitiveness or the need to prove yourself worthy by having more than another, then can you see that you will be setting yourself up for a lesson in humanity?

Many partially understand that they get more by helping others. I have seen those who openly advocate that you will get what you want by being of service. However, if the reason for that is for your own success with the intention to prove your value and to be better than others, then at some point the underlying lack of self-worth will need to be resolved. When it is though, a whole new level is reached.

It may be that your compassion inspires you to build a business that furthers humanity as well as have the resources to enable you to continue to live and experience this world in its entirety. You may want to develop skills that will allow you to share your growing awareness with those who can benefit. Or perhaps you want to share your home with others who need your gifts.

All through this book, we have been focusing on you, your self-care and your self-understanding. As this grows so does your compassion for others, which, in turn, leads you to desire to help them too. We said right at the beginning that putting yourself at the top of the list is not selfish, and this is why. We have come full circle.

Taking the Steps

Now you have your vision board and mind map, it is time to break what you want down into manageable steps to get you where you want to be.

Work backwards from your goal, so you can see what you need to do, and so you can build a timetable to achieve it.

If you want to be a teacher, for example, and your research tells you that you require, say, one year of training, you will also need to allow time to prepare your application to the college before the beginning of the course. You may need to get further qualifications before you can start, so build that in, too. You will then have a timeline of how you are going to reach your goal and the steps you need to take along the way to get there. It may seem a long way away, but know that you have drifted away from your dreams, and it is now time to get back to where you want to be. It is never too late. I cannot emphasise this enough. The journey is the destination, so enjoy getting to where you want to be as much as getting there. There is immense joy, as well as relief, in knowing your life is on track and that you are heading where you want to go.

You may decide you want to change your vision as your life develops. That's fine. None of this is fixed in stone.

In my experience, nothing is wasted. It is as if the universe can utilise it all. All the life experiences you have had and the struggles and successes you have experienced will be used. If your dream is to be a teacher, I would like to bet you will be a fantastic teacher for being able to bring to your students all the incredible life learning and experiences that have shown you so much.

Developing your vision for your life enables you to move more into its flow. You will feel more connected to it, and changes will begin, possibly gently and subtly at first, then with more significant and often surprising developments. It gets inspiring and is so worth making an effort for.

If you can bring all these steps together, you will inevitably move towards both living your full potential and living your life purpose.

But there's one last step you need to take that is essential to keep all of this excitement on track to achieve the results you want, and this is what we will look at in the next chapter.

Summary

- Tap into your inner guidance to get where you want to be.
- Master the tools of creation: thoughts, words, actions, and feelings.
- Cover the basics and then allow yourself to dream big for your life.
- Self-care develops compassion for both the self and for others.
- Include this compassion in your vision.

Main Action Steps

1. Mindmap your desires.
2. Create a vision board to reflect that.
3. Create a timeline for achieving it.

The Result

Your life becomes one of joy.

CHAPTER SIX

The Fifth Key: Reach Out

No man is an island, entire of itself; every man is a piece of the continent, a part of the main.
– John Donne

Friendship … is born at the moment when one person says to another "What! You too? I thought that no one but myself…"
– C. S. Lewis

It's OK to Have Help and Support to Get to the Good Stuff and Find Love.

You have read about the keys to get the life you want, and you know what you need to do. But there is one big problem with everything we have covered so far.

That problem is that it's not easy to do on your own.

You might be able to do some of it for a day, a week, or perhaps even for a month, but without support, accountability, guidance, and like-minded friendship, you are highly likely to slip back into old habits, old ways of thinking and the path you were on before.

No one ever lived their life or took these steps alone. Nor are you meant to. To maintain your practices, to keep you living your dreams on a daily basis, to create the life you want, and do it fast, you are going to need support and guidance.

Take New Year's resolutions, for example. A significant number don't make it past the first week, and around 50% don't make it past the first month. These resolutions were quite possibly made at the last minute, in isolation, and without a programme of support and accountability. They are not necessarily doomed to fail, but the statistics show failure is highly likely. People who explicitly make resolutions, in other words, who are very conscious about what they want to do and how they want to do it, are ten times more likely to attain their goals than people who don't explicitly make resolutions.

Without support and some form of accountability, you are in danger of getting confused and overwhelmed. It is a short step from there to losing your direction; you can slip seamlessly off track, from where it all seems too much, and you give up.

Giving up means not only will you be accepting less than you deserve, but also giving up on all the beautiful things that are waiting for you – and I promise you they are waiting for you.

On the other hand, when you invest in yourself by seeking support, it shows your subconscious your determination to make changes, by sending out a message that the downward spiral, the stuckness must stop. Enough is enough.

Aim for the support that will guide you past the boulders and pebbles that usually trip people up. Look for help to avoid going down dead-ends and getting waylaid. You want support that keeps you on the right path to make progress fast. Proper support will help you avoid overwhelm and give you resources to guide you. Surround yourself with people that will both physically and emotionally support you, be a sounding board for your ideas and help keep you on your path. Motivational speaker Jim Rohn famously said that we are the average of the five people we spend the most time with, so choose your inner circle carefully.

The best form of support will guide you to move on, shed the past, and only bring forward from it that which serves you.

As your life situation changes, you may find that your friendships change. You have possibly found that out already. Your new status will threaten some people. It might be because they fear the same might happen to them, and they don't want to be reminded of it, or they don't know how your new relationship status fits in with their existing friendship group and view of the world. It might be because they see the pain it is causing and feel that they can't handle it. Whatever the reason, hopefully, it is clear that if they drift away, it is their issue, not yours.

You, however, will want to grow and develop. You wouldn't have got this far in this book if you didn't. Allow any changes in friendships to happen naturally and peacefully. As you follow the keys towards the life of your choosing, you will find people will come in who are more aligned with your life as it grows and develops. These are the people who will want to share with you and be there for you.

As we drop our conditioning, so the barriers between us fall. This means you will find yourself developing more in-depth and more meaningful relationships than possibly you ever thought achievable.

Accountability

One excellent way to help you keep moving forward is to have an accountability partner, someone to help keep you focussed and on track. A like-minded person is best suited for this, someone with whom you can mutually grow and share. If you know someone who might be interested, maybe you can give them a copy of this book, so you are both coming from the same place. Or even share a few free pages that you can find here:

www.helpyourcellves.com/free-pages

More Help for You

It is invaluable to have one or more friends who are on the same journey as you and who understand what you are working on. If they want the same for themselves too, that is even better.

Hear what Katie P. had to say:

> 'I came to [Sara] because I was feeling heartbroken, defeated, and utterly confused as to the right way forward. I was paralysed with indecision, and every time I tried to solve my problems, things seemed to go badly wrong. I had been struggling on my own for months to come to terms with the end of my marriage. Friends offered tea and sympathy and advice influenced by their own experiences, but that was contradictory and left me more confused than ever.

> 'Sara immediately provided me with a defined structure and framework to stabilise me and give me the tools I needed to find my way forward.'

If you want to move on fast and effectively with more personal guidance, then you might also like to take a look at The Phoenix Programme, designed to empower women to both heal the pain and rise from the ashes of breakup and embrace the new life of their choosing.

https://helpyourcellves.com/divorce-coaching/

You can also join our private Facebook group for more support and conversations with like-minded new friends.

https://www.facebook.com/groups/DivorceBeGoneLetsMoveOn/

Summary

- You are not meant to struggle on alone.
- Support will help you avoid falling by the wayside.
- If you fall by the wayside, you lose out on the bounty that awaits you.
- Getting support helps you get where you want to be.

Main Action Steps

1. Consider The Phoenix Programme to empower you.

2. Get an accountability friend so you can share the journey (and this book).
3. Join the private Facebook group for support and community.
4. Let me know how it all goes.

The Result

You open your life up to more love.

Conclusion

The aim of this book has been to show you how you can change your life around no matter what point you are starting from. It is never too late nor beyond your ability because you have the power over your own life.

Using the Five Keys given here will mean you can unlock the immense potential you have to experience an amazing life. You most likely didn't know the power you have because no one even told you that you had it, let alone how to use it to create what you want.

However, it is not possible to access this power if your self-worth and self-esteem are low or non-existent. For this reason, we began with Key One which highlights the importance of valuing you and how self-care and self-respect are where to start.

We then looked at Key Two, new ways of looking at what is happening to you with fresh eyes. Understanding situations in a different way opens your life to new possibilities and ways of being so you can leave behind the drama and conflict and find peace.

Key Three is all about getting to the root cause of why you are in the situation you are in so patterns no longer repeat.

We looked at where it all went wrong and why, and then what you can do to turn it around.

This means you are then free to access Key Four, which is about how to develop and work towards the life you really want.

Finally, Key Five gives you permission to get support and not struggle on alone. We are meant to work, live, love and grow together, so it's only fitting to have the support you need along the way. Choose wisely here and your life and joy will expand exponentially.

You create your world by your thoughts, words, feelings, and actions. All four are critical. In other words, for things to change, you need to take purposeful action, fed by thoughts, words, and feelings focused on the direction you want. This is where the magic happens, and it is from here you will move on to the life you desire.

Although the process is simple, it isn't always easy. There will be challenges. But by keeping your focus on the Five Keys we have covered, you will see your life move forward in a way you never thought possible when you were in the depths of despair.

You are the most important person in your life, and I wish you all the success in the world, as you make your reality one of your own choosing.

I would love to hear how things progress for you, so please message me with any feedback or questions https://helpyourcellves.com/contact/

FINALLY…

As I write the last few words of this book, I am aware of how much I have drawn from my own experience over the years. There have been many changes of direction, and many of my ventures have been what some might call failure. It has been a winding and often rocky road to where I am now, with more ups and downs than a long roller coaster ride. Yet, here I am, writing to you about it all, having distilled my experience of moving on from divorce into the keys that I know will also enable you to be where you want if you take action on them.

I couldn't have written this book two years ago, let alone 10 years ago. In fact, at the time of writing the first draft of this paragraph, it was only three weekends ago that I decided to overcome my long-held belief that I couldn't write a book. And here you are holding my book in your hands or reading it on your device. That is how quickly things can change.

Keep challenging those beliefs now that you can see where they come from because you are more than you ever imagined you could be. By doing that for yourself, the journey will progress, and life will continue to expand beyond what you ever thought possible.

It's tough being on your own after a relationship has ended. It's also tough being lonely and taken for granted within a relationship. So, put yourself centre-stage of your own life, and hop on the ride.

You never know quite where that ride will take you and that's the fun of it. We have been given so much by being able to live on this amazing and bountiful planet, and, with the keys in this book, you can develop your own abundant life in reflection of that. Foster your connection with your inner guidance, and you will have the best friend you could ever wish for. For life!

You are a gift to yourself and to the world, and my greatest wish for you is that you find your freedom to expand, grow, love your life and shine your light.

Love always,

Sara

Acknowledgements

Thank you to my parents for doing their very best for me and always being there. Mum, you were and are my biggest teacher, enabling me to learn about myself, and grow. Dad, you have always given me constant and unwavering support, and your passion and love of life is an inspiration.

Susie, Kim and Freddie, you have brought so much joy into my life just by being you. I love you more than words can say.

Mike Robinson and Jo Le-Rose, for your constancy in pointing the way to true love, and then letting me discover love's depths for myself. You are always in my heart.

A special mention for all my amazing, fantastic friends both in the UK, and all over the world, with whom I am sharing this incredible journey of life. With every year our love grows and deepens, and I couldn't be more thankful to have you all in my life.

Finally a massive appreciation to all those who have supported me as I've written this book, and to those who are helping share its very existence. You are absolute stars. Thank you.

About the Author

Sara Gibbons has been a natural health practitioner and lifestyle strategist for over 20 years, successfully helping hundreds of clients improve and move on in their lives. She has a degree in sociology, and extensive training, experience and qualifications in counselling, nutrition and personal development. Along the way she has learned a variety of other healing therapies and disciplines, set up and run her own natural therapy centre, and worked at a Spa and Retreat in Central France.

Born and bred in North London, Sara has also lived in and worked in the Midlands and the North of the UK. Now in Norfolk she is delighted to be fulfilling a lifelong dream to live close to the sea. She decided it was time to share her knowledge, knowing that the solutions she brings to her writing are also born of personal experience. There are plans to follow her first book, Rise Again After Divorce, with others in a Help Your Cellves Empowerment series on health, work, and more…

You can find more about Sara and her work here:

www.helpyourcellves.com

Thank You for Reading this Book!

Can you help?

I really appreciate receiving feedback and hearing what you have to say.

Your input helps me improve the next version of this book and future books.

Please leave a helpful review on Amazon letting me know what you thought of it.

Thank you so much!

Sara Gibbons

Made in the USA
Las Vegas, NV
01 March 2025

18866849R00066